D1567157

Legendary LIONEL® TRAINS

John A. Grams &
Terry D. Thompson

KALMBACH
BOOKS

ACKNOWLEDGMENTS

No one ever really writes a book without help, of course. Even if a book has two authors, as this one does, those authors undoubtedly received help, ideas, encouragement, and inspiration from others as well as from each other. We know we did.

So, in no particular order, we would like to thank: Cindy and Marin Thompson, who sat gamely through many hours of our conversations about Lionel in general and this book in particular, cheering us on all the while; Dick Christianson of *Model Railroader*, who encouraged us to start this project and whose gentle good nature and steady friendship helped us persevere to the end; Roger Carp, Bob Keller, and Neil Besougloff of *Classic Toy Trains*, who helped us refine our ideas; Kent Johnson, who is not only our editor but a trusted friend and colleague; Kristi Ludwig, William Zuback, and especially Jim Forbes, whose artistic creativity enriched the project in so many ways; Jack Sommerfeld, Tom Palmer Jr., Richard Kughn, and John Wickland, who generously lent us many items from their collections; and Terral Klaassen and Dale Schafer, who were always willing to talk trains—even at a drag race.

Most of all, though, we would like to thank our parents, uncles, and grandparents, who introduced us to toy trains (at very different times and places, of course), and in so doing not only kindled a friendship between a boy from Sheboygan, Wisconsin, and one from Elyria, Ohio, but changed our lives forever. We're both the better for it. It's safe to say that we have indeed enjoyed every trip we took at the throttle of our trains.

About the photographs in this book: Many of them come from the absolutely priceless *Classic Toy Trains* collection. The remainder were shot for the book by Jim Forbes and William Zuback at the Kalmbach Publishing Co. photo studio. We would like to thank Kalmbach for giving us access to the collection, and we would also like to thank all the *Classic Toy Trains* staff members and photographers (including Bill and Jim plus Chris Becker, Darla Evans, Rebecca Saliture, and Art Schmidt) who have done such good work over the years. Thanks also to Joe Algozzini and Paul Wasserman for lending some of the items shown in this book to *Classic Toy Trains*.

Published by Kalmbach Trade Press, a division of Kalmbach Publishing Co., 21027 Crossroads Circle, Waukesha, WI 53186-1612. These books are distributed to the book trade by Watson-Guptill.

Printed in People's Republic of China

04 05 06 07 08 09 10 11 12   10 9 8 7 6 5 4 3 2 1

Publisher's Cataloging-in-Publication
(Provided by Quality Books, Inc.)

Grams, John.
    Legendary Lionel Trains / John A. Grams, Terry D.
Thompson.
    p. cm.
    ISBN 0-87116-211-3

    1. Railroads—Models. 2. Lionel Corporation.
I. Thompson, Terry (Terry D.) II. Title.

TF197.G6415 2004   625.1'9
                          QBI04-200193

Art Director: Kristi Ludwig

TABLE OF CONTENTS

Legendary Lionel Trains

Early 8	*Golden Era 38*	*Contemporary 116*
A century ago, Joshua Lionel Cowen started a company to make eye-catching window displays. He ended up producing the legendary Standard and O gauge trains that established Lionel as America's leading toy train company.	Beginning in 1937, Lionel offered a line of trains and accessories that allowed young engineers to create spectacular miniature worlds. These trains fostered millions of memories and made Lionel the world's largest toy company.	By the 1970s American boys wanted other toys, and model trains looked a bit out-of-date. But with the help of adult hobbyists, modern technology, and some great new models, Lionel made a dramatic comeback.

PREFACE

When we formulated the idea for this book, we thought it would be a simple project: A few months of talking and taking notes about trains, a few more months to develop those notes from an outline into a manuscript, and a few months to find photos. We figured nine months, tops. That was eight years ago.

We kept going because we were convinced that the Lionel story deserved a book that would share that story with all of us who enjoyed a Lionel during our childhoods. For that reason, we've deliberately avoided catalog numbers, condition ratings, estimates of rarity, and the other train-enthusiast terms.

Instead, we've concentrated on those facets—size, color, action, and much more—of the trains that made Lionel products icons of childhood and American culture. Once upon a time Lionel was just a company, but today, more than a century after its founding, it has become an institution. Lionel toy trains have become part of our shared American story, especially at Christmas.

And the trains themselves? They've become legends. —*Terry D. Thompson*

PROLOGUE

Electricity was the new wonder of the world at the turn of the twentieth century. The mere mention of the word conjured images of a better, brighter way of life in the future. Although some of its properties had been known for a long time, few outside of the scientific community and those lucky enough to be living in the wealthier sections of large cities had any first-hand experience with it.

The most popular and awe-inspiring spectacle at the avant-garde St. Louis Exposition of 1903 was an "electric waterfall," the perceived motion of which was created by a bank of several hundred light bulbs, blinking sequentially against the night sky. People gaped at it for hours. Few could imagine the impact the energy that powered this novelty would soon have on their lives .

At the same time, the railroads in America were in the midst of great expansion, both geographically and technologically. Parallel ribbons of steel already linked the country from border to border and coast to coast. The great trunk line railroads were adding branches and improving service, while smaller regional lines were finding their niches. Trains were in the news almost every day.

The sight of locomotive smoke on the horizon and the sound of distant whistles had become symbols of American industrial strength and the lure of faraway places. The dream had no down side. Even the soot, cinders, rumble, and racket that the trains produced were viewed as "romantic." Railroad engineers, who piloted mighty steam locomotives, were fast becoming folk heroes, the subjects of story and song, to be idolized by the young.

Parents encouraged this, hoping that their offspring might choose railroading as a career. Others saw the occupational potential in the electrical field. The two fields—trains and electricity—became truly magical when combined. Boys who couldn't wait to become men were totally captivated, but had to be content with their toys—for a while.

By 1900, kid-powered toy locomotives of the push-and-pull variety had been popular for 40 years. Self-propelled clockwork (windup) trains, pioneered in Europe, had been around for a decade—some even had their own tracks. A small American company had experimented with battery-powered electric motors in toy trolley cars a few years before.

Then came Lionel. The firm's founder, Joshua Lionel Cowen, didn't invent toy trains or put the first motors in them. Yet his company, through a combination of vision, ingenuity, and marketing, became the world's largest toy train manufacturer. Indeed, the name "Lionel" has been a synonym—almost a generic term—for electric trains for more than a century.

Therein lies the legend. *—John A. Grams*

INTRODUCTION

It wasn't supposed to happen like this, of course. Joshua Lionel Cowen was an inventor of electrical devices back when electricity was the most magical technology of the age. Making everything from fans to flashlights, he tinkered and tweaked, experimented and expounded. He was a Renaissance Man of the Age of Electricity, not a specialist, and he didn't start out intending to enter the toy business. His "Electric Express" wasn't even meant to be a toy—he sold the first models to retailers for use as an attention-getter in their store windows. His invention was meant to carry the items retailers most wanted to market.

But instead of clamoring for the dolls, razors, or watches riding in the little cigar-box-sized gondola, customers wanted to buy the train itself. More by accident than by design, Cowen found himself in the toy business. Eventually, he would become its king.

He wasn't the first to make toy trains, of course, and for many years his little company was just that—little. But the same restless, relentless energy that had led him to become an inventor in the first place gave his company an edge over its competitors that it has never relinquished. Sure, some years were better for Lionel than others, and it's even likely that every now and then another American company sold more trains than Lionel in a given year.

No other train company, however, has ever approached the place Lionel holds in the American imagination. In fact, to find companies that enjoy similar levels of public awareness you have to go up several weight classes, to firms like Harley-Davidson, Kodak, and Chevrolet. A century after its founding, "Lionel" still means "model train" to most Americans. Lionel around the tree has become every bit as much a part of the American myth as Mom's apple pie or Santa Claus in the Thanksgiving Day parade.

Over time, of course, the company has changed, and so have both the market for its products and the way it marketed those products. In its early years, Lionel was on the leading edge of technology and its products were purchased mainly by the well-to-do. It marketed those trains as forward-looking, high-tech toys.

By the 1940s and '50s, Lionel technology was still very good, contemporary with much of American industry if perhaps no longer the source of wonder. The marketing pitch Lionel chose shifted subtly; now its core message was that trains would bring fathers and sons together so that Dad could prepare Junior for the world of work.

After some lean years in the 1960s and early '70s, Lionel came roaring back. This time it seemed the largest part of its market consisted of nostalgic adults who were hoping to relive a childhood memory or two. These consumers didn't mind that the company's technology was now behind the times. In fact, they liked it that way. The new marketing pitch echoed the thought that these trains and sets were products with a long heritage, and the word "collectible" began to appear frequently. Reissues of its most legendary items brought good times to Lionel, and the firm was happy to let those good times roll.

Today, after an infusion of creative energy by enthusiasts Richard Kughn and Neil Young, among others, Lionel trains are high-tech again. Their digital sound and control systems allow operators to re-create every facet of a real railroad operation. And who buys them? Well, many products still go to nostalgic adults. It's not by coincidence that some of the best-selling Lionel items are models of steam locomotives, and the bigger the locomotive the better.

But many Lionel trains go to people who aren't looking to re-create their childhoods and who don't see a train as a way to prepare someone for a career. Instead, they go to people who are hoping that building a layout will enrich the lives of their children or grandchildren—and wouldn't mind a respite from their own busy careers as well. The idea of a Lionel still resonates because it suggests a simpler time and family togetherness. It may not sound very Generation Y, but it still works.

Even given all the brilliant marketing strategies in the world, though, Lionel wouldn't have survived a decade, much less a century, if the trains weren't good. Their construction is so sturdy, in fact, that 25-, 50-, even 75-year-old Lionel trains still run on layouts all across the country. Until the advent of the new generation of Lionel models, one of the firm's biggest competitors was itself, in the form of the hundreds of thousands of serviceable trains that were still in circulation. Imagine if Chevrolet had to sell its cars into a market in which hundreds of thousands of 1957 Chevys still provided perfectly reliable daily transportation.

The newest (not the oldest—the newest!) Lionel locomotive that either of us currently owns is from 1955. If we want to run Lionel trains, we have to trust that our 50-year-old engines will run. They always do.

Lionel trains new and old not only run reliably, but they fire imaginations too. People of all ages still line up to watch them run, whether on a public display or a home layout. Folks may not make their Thanksgiving journey to Grandmother's house via train any more, but they still enjoy seeing models of the trains they rode back in those days.

Even more than that, however, parents and grandparents love pointing at a Lionel and exclaiming, "That's just like the one I had when I was your age!" In doing so, they're sharing the legend with another generation. As we think you'll agree, the Lionel legend is worth sharing. *—John A. Grams and Terry D. Thompson*

Early LIONEL TRAINS ®

These days, we feel lucky if one of our appliances—a mixer, say, or an answering machine—lasts five years. Sure, the prices are right, but forget about passing it along to your son or daughter, let alone a grandchild.

If you place a Lionel train from 1930 (or 1920 or 1910, for that matter) on the track and apply power, it will almost always run. It may be rusty, dented, or missing a few parts, but its heart will still be strong. These trains were built in a time when durability and longevity were not merely advertising slogans. They remain mirrors of an era when electricity was a wonder and American industry was the envy of the world.

Back then, parents wanted their boys to have a Lionel because it would teach them lessons they could use when they went out to make their way in the world. Their boys wanted a Lionel because they knew that running the powerful locomotive would make them feel like men. Now, nearly 100 years later, Americans of all ages want old Lionel trains because they're colorful, beautiful, and valuable reflections of the culture of a past era, just like other fine antiques.

NEW CENTURY, NEW COMPANY

1900-1925

Working in a small loft on New York's Murray Street, Joshua Lionel Cowen and his partner considered themselves inventors and product developers. Others probably called them "tinkerers." With several electrical patents in their portfolio, they were at work on an improved dry-cell battery and a small, cool-running motor. After a disagreement, Cowen's partner left with the battery patents and started the Eveready Flashlight business. Cowen then named his own operation The Lionel Manufacturing Company.

As the story goes, Mr. Cowen was strolling about the neighborhood in 1900, window-shopping as he considered his next ventures. He noticed that passers-by paid little attention to the static merchandise displays. Something moving in the shop windows might change this, he thought. Why not a motorized car on a circle of track? Small items or signs announcing specials could be carried in it.

So he put his little motor into a wooden gondola car which ran on strap steel track with an odd gauge—2⅞ inches.

Customers still paid no attention to the merchandise for sale. Instead, they all wanted to buy the wooden gondola car. Everyone in the store played with the thing.

When the first Lionel catalog was printed in 1901, the wooden gondola car was named "Electric Express" and was

the running rails and a whole new line of trains to go with it. In front was a four-wheel-drive locomotive mechanism with realistic spoked wheels and a reversing lever. It was initially installed into two steam locomotives that had the look of American prototypes of the day.

Later, the mechanism was used in electric-profile engines as well.

No fewer than six freight cars and three passenger cars were featured in the catalog. All were of durable, soldered sheet-metal construction and equipped with a pair of realistically swiveling four-wheel trucks. Of course, there were also trolley cars, available as motorized units or trailers. Soon, new electric-profile locomotives, like those frequently seen on Eastern railroads, took their places alongside the steamers. The colors of these early Lionel trains, although varied, were rather dull and earthy—imitating those commonly encountered on the real railroads.

Another landmark year for Lionel occurred in 1910. The company began packaging some trains in sets, consisting of locomotive, cars, and track. The company labeled these unique sets "outfits."

A series of longer cars was introduced to go along with the new larger engines in the premium sets. From that time on, Lionel always made rolling stock in at least two sizes per gauge, to match the mass of the locomotives.

As the company's market base expanded to include middle-income train buyers in addition to the more affluent

joined by a trolley car labeled "City Hall Park." These were the first train-related Lionel products. By 1905, Cowen's small loft factory had also turned out a tunnel locomotive and three other cars.

Incompatibilities abounded in the fledgling toy train industry. The products of one manufacturer usually would not work with those of another. Nowhere was this problem more acute than with track gauge. Cowen felt that if the industry were to grow, there had to be a standardized track gauge, so he lobbied the other manufacturers to adopt one.

In 1906, Lionel took a bold step by announcing "Lionel Standard Gauge" three-rail track, with 2¼ inches between ones, physical space became a real consideration. Chances were these people didn't have large parlors, spare rooms, or attics that could be devoted to their children's playtime. Introducing a smaller train line seemed a logical next step.

With relatively little fanfare, Lionel entered the O gauge field (1¼ inches between running rails) in 1915. Obviously, Standard was still the company's primary gauge and commanded the most ink in the catalog. The new O gauge trains were made in the image of their ancestors—only they were smaller. The colors were the same, car for car, because they were dipped into the same paint vats.

All the early O gauge locomotives were of electric profile, based loosely on a New York Central prototype. Most had operating headlights and an oversized, two-piece bell detail. The better ones featured manual reverse levers. Dark green was the color of choice, with rubber-stamped gold lettering.

As with Standard gauge, there were two sizes of freight and passenger cars in O gauge. The smaller series were four-wheelers, the larger cars had swiveling trucks, and the deluxe passenger cars sported interior lighting.

Lionel incorporated in 1918. In the aftermath of the First World War, times were good economically, particularly during the "Roaring" 1920s. Sales volume at Lionel mushroomed with the boom in discretionary spending. The O gauge line started to gather steam.

Lionel moved production from the little loft to other locations in New York City before taking over an empty factory building in Irvington, New Jersey. Business was so brisk that this, too, proved inadequate to handle projected growth. So plans were drawn up to build a large, modern plant on a spacious plot of land between Hillside and Irvington in New Jersey. (It was completed in 1929.) The main office, corporate headquarters, and showroom remained in Manhattan.

To the advantage of Lionel, significant urban electrification had been accomplished by the middle of the 1920s, as power companies began building facilities in even the smaller cities. Wiring the hinterlands and rural areas would take more time and federal aid. Meanwhile, Lionel was retooling, sharpening its product image, and heading for a truly mass market.

Electric Express gondola
City Hall Park trolley car

The earliest Lionel legend of all revolves around this 15-inch wooden gondola car, which was the first electrically propelled vehicle made by Joshua Lionel Cowen in his New York City loft, circa 1900. Cowen had developed a small, reliable electric motor and needed something to demonstrate it.

According to the accepted folklore, his idea was to market these cars, along with a circle of track and a storage battery, to shopkeepers as a means of animating their usually static window displays. It worked, perhaps too well! Store employees spent time playing with the cars and customers wanted to buy them.

Unfortunately for the store owners, nobody cared about the other merchandise displayed in their windows.

By 1901, when the first simple Lionel catalog was printed, the gondola had been joined by a metal trolley car in the lineup. Lionel was on its way to becoming the world's largest toy train manufacturer.

Interestingly enough, Lionel made only the motors and drive mechanisms. The car bodies were produced by outside vendors. The trolley came from the Converse Company, a firm that made large windup floor toys. The gondola bodies were purchased from a manufacturer of wooden cheese boxes.

Early Standard gauge freight train

The Lionel deluxe Standard gauge 4-4-0 steam locomotive of the early period had the appearance of many "iron horses" that were used by American railroads during the first decades of the twentieth century. It was sturdily constructed of heavy gauge sheet metal and cast iron and featured spoked drivers, a working headlight, realistic side and piston rods, an ornamental bell, and a manual reverse lever. The same reliable four-wheel-drive motor mechanism was used in all Lionel locomotives—both steam and electric profile—during the period.

The cars that are shown here—five of the six in the larger series of Standard gauge freight haulers (only the gondola is missing)—were also made of soldered sheet metal. They sported extra details that workers at Lionel attached by hand.

All of these popular models tracked well, thanks to the two swiveling and articulated trucks that were installed under each of them. These basic freight cars with only some minor variations were cataloged by Lionel for almost 20 years.

Early Standard gauge electric locomotive

This Standard gauge replica of a New York Central electric-profile locomotive was almost 16 inches long and featured twin motors to give it exceptional pulling power. Lionel was the first toy train manufacturer to use a two-motored configuration to increase traction instead of simply adding weight to the engine, as some competitors did.

The catalog for 1922 boasted that this electric locomotive could pull "twenty of our largest freight cars or a dozen of our largest passenger cars with perfect ease." It probably could, although few young operators at the time owned enough rolling stock to put the engine to the test.

1915 O gauge set

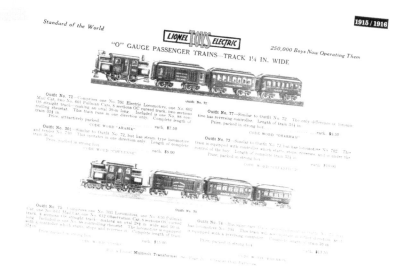

This is literally the first O gauge train Lionel ever made, vintage 1915. All evidence points to it being the handmade prototype model from which the pre-production catalog picture was drawn.

While the 4-4-4 electric-profile locomotive and the Pullman and observation cars are well documented in toy train literature and reside in several private collections, the four-door mail car is presumed to have been cataloged but not manufactured.

Other subtle differences, such as the number of window pairs in the Pullman and observation cars (five instead of the usual six) and the externally braced locomotive trucks, lead to the conclusion that this was the train put together months ahead of the regular production run so the artist could meet the catalog deadline.

All the components of this set match the picture perfectly, but differ from the known units that were mass-produced. Then there's the baggage and mail car—this is likely the only one ever made.

The toy train collector who now owns this unique treasure says he bought it a few years ago from someone who had owned it for a long time and didn't remember where or when he acquired it. Here this train's legend ends and its mystery begins.

DECADE OF COLOR, DECADE OF CHALLENGE

1926-1936

Many Standard gauge train collectors refer to this decade as the "Classic Period" or the "Brass Plate Era." It represented a wholesale revision of the entire Lionel line—including both Standard and O gauges—accomplished with much fanfare and publicity over several years. The changes began about 1923 and took four years to complete. The evolutionary process Lionel used not only allowed for the slow phasing in of new tooling, but also provided for the complete liquidation of old inventory. As a result, many interesting "transitional" sets were created in the interim.

There had been a sameness to the look of Lionel trains for years. Many of the railroad prototypes used for the first Standard gauge products dated to the 1890s. By the 1920s the toys were starting to look quaint. The revisions that took place were intended to improve the line and bring it up-to-date.

Early casualties in this extreme makeover were the two Standard gauge steam locomotives. Most of the toy train companies, including Lionel, were promoting electric-profile engines anyway because they were seen as cutting-edge technology at the time. So, for four years Lionel was all-electric in both gauges. The old-style juice hogs were gradually phased out, replaced by more modern-looking models of New York Central, Pennsylvania, and Milwaukee Road prototypes. To keep more inquisitive youngsters occupied,

Lionel offered one of its new Standard gauge electrics in simple kit form. Called "Bild-A-Loco," the engine was intended to be taken apart and reassembled over and over again. It came with instructions to show its owner how to do it correctly. The motor could also be used to power other toys. What an educational experience! It might keep Junior from taking apart the lamp or the toaster.

The new sheet-metal locomotives and cars featured a different type of construction. Tabs and slots replaced the old assembly method of soldering the pieces together. The corners were rounded and the edges rolled, so there were no sharp exposed surfaces to accidentally injure anyone. This was an important feature, since almost everything in the Lionel catalog was made from stamped steel.

Two sizes of rolling stock, as designated by numerical series, remained in Standard and O gauges. This time the differences were accompanied by variations in coupler height, making it difficult to mix the series.

Manually operated freight cars, such as cranes, dump cars, and floodlight cars, could be found in both gauges.

Specialty outfits, like work trains and coal-hauling unit trains, were offered for the first time. Passenger cars, except for those in a few low-end starter sets, had interior illumination.

Much greater attention was paid to details. Embossed rivets could be found in all the appropriate places. Shiny metal railings, pipes, bells, brake wheels, and ladders were added by hand. Top-of-the-line Standard gauge passenger cars had seats and lavatories. Every locomotive and car had brass name and number plates attached.

Colors became brighter and glossier as Lionel baked on its automotive-grade enamel. The new construction method allowed individual pieces to be painted before final assembly, so two-tone and combination color schemes were easy to accomplish.

As the era progressed, the colors gradually became more brilliant (some might say loud and gaudy) by design. Apparently, Cowen's research had indicated that although intended as gifts for boys, most toy train purchases were made by women—mothers, grandmothers, aunts, and the like. He thought that if he cranked up the colors, his trains would be more appealing to their primary buyers. That theory eventually ran its course, but not before the rainbow had been exhausted.

At the beginning of 1926, all motive power in both gauges was of the electric type. After the new generation of steamers was introduced—in 1929 for Standard gauge and 1930 for O gauge—the emphasis rapidly shifted toward them. More were added each year until the Lionel roundhouse was full of the new steamers. Undoubtedly, Lionel was trying to broaden its customer base beyond the electrified Northeast Corridor to other parts of the country where steam power was primary. The most important advances in scale/toy locomotive technology in this period were the automatic

better Lionel steam locomotives in 1935. By 1936, it was an available option on every train in the line. The addition of this realistic sound effect was a big hit with young engineers, although it probably drove many parents crazy. The built-in motorized whistle also remained intact for decades, until electronic circuits, computer chips, and tiny speakers took over.

Lionel's experiments with high-pressure metal die-casting techniques for small parts and components in this era led to the introduction of the complete, highly detailed die-cast locomotive bodies that would become the company's hallmark in the eras that followed. Investment in the necessary equipment paid for itself many times over.

Big-time passenger trains were center stage. Many of them had important-sounding names, like *Transcontinental Limited*, *Blue Comet*, and *Broadway Limited* in Standard gauge, and *Hiawatha*, *Red Comet*, *Flying Yankee*, and *City of Denver* (M-10000) in O gauge. Some of these names were drawn from the real world, while others were made-up.

Operating trackside accessories were introduced during these years. On these, lights blinked, gates went down, warning bells rang, semaphore arms raised and lowered, and that all-time favorite gateman came out of his shanty to wave his lantern and warn motorists that a train was approaching. While most of these accessories were initially advertised as appropriate for both O and Standard gauge, many of the larger ones were scaled down or eliminated completely when O became the primary Lionel gauge.

sequence-reversing mechanism, the built-in whistle, and the utilization of high-pressure die-casting techniques.

While most toy locomotives had been reversible from the beginning (done by manipulating a lever on the engine), the development of a remote-control device that automatically changed the direction of the train wasn't undertaken until the mid-1920s. An interruption of the track power triggered it.

At first, Lionel reversers had only two positions—forward and backward. The now-familiar three-position sequence, with a neutral mode in between, didn't appear until 1930, when Lionel took over the assets and patents of the bankrupt Ives Manufacturing Corporation, its developer. The new reverse unit soon became a staple in Lionel locomotives on all levels. It remained until the dawn of the age of electronic reversing controls in the 1990s.

A motor-driven air whistle which could be activated at any point on the track layout began appearing in the tenders of

The stock market disaster of 1929 and the national economic depression it engendered were by far the largest determinants for Lionel in this period of change, as they were for many other businesses that had to paddle hard to stay afloat. After a brief period of receivership, Lionel bailed itself out primarily by competing in the lower arenas of the marketplace with $1.00 novelties and $1.50 windup and $3.25 tin-lithographed electric trains—while trying to maintain the integrity, image, and price points of its regular line that started at $6.00 or $7.00 and topped out at $97.50.

The 1930 and 1931 catalogs were the company's largest to that date with 36 outfits equally divided between O and Standard gauge. Using the number of sets in the catalog as a measure, a sharp downward spiral began after 1932. It continued in O gauge until 1936, when there was a slight upturn. Standard gauge kept on sliding to its eventual demise in 1939.

While many observers probably questioned the wisdom of the Ives takeover in 1930, it may have been a key factor in the survival of Lionel. First of all, it eliminated a competitor. The superior Ives reversing mechanism strengthened the Lionel line without adding to its price. Making another line of trains more efficiently utilized the production capabilities of the new factory. Acquiring an existing customer base and a line of inexpensive windup and electric trains gave Lionel a solid footing to deal with its only remaining competitor, American Flyer Manufacturing Company, based in Chicago. The Ives line

remained intact until 1932. Some "Lionel-Ives" outfits appeared in the 1933 Lionel catalog. The name was changed to "Lionel Junior" in 1934. By 1937, these low-end sets had become the "O-27" line and the assimilation was complete.

Meanwhile, in searching for new potential groups of train consumers, Lionel discovered that the affluent scale model railroad hobbyists were largely under-served. The Union Pacific *M-10000* and the Milwaukee Road *Hiawatha* streamliners were the company's first attempts at entering this market. Conquering it would soon become a major thrust.

So, as Lionel entered the next phase, which we have called "realism and rejuvenation," Standard gauge was on the way out, O gauge was again on the rise, and Lionel Junior trains were providing a popular lower-priced alternative. State-of-the-art streamliners were big. A perceived new market among scale model railroaders and the influence of that perception would soon have a remarkable effect on Lionel product design and appearance at all levels.

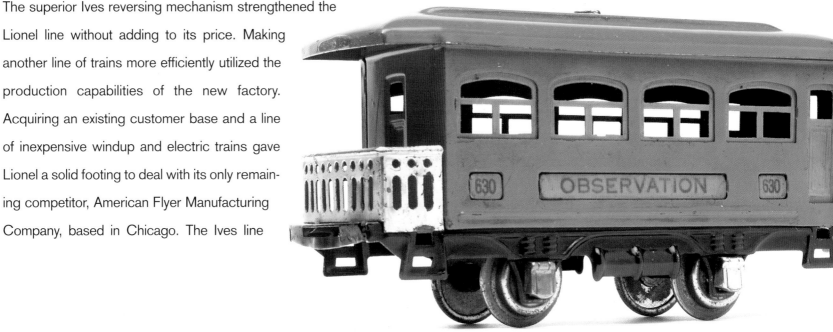

The *Blue Comet*

The *Blue Comet* was the Central Railroad of New Jersey's deluxe excursion train that shuttled revelers and fun seekers from Jersey City and New York to the Atlantic City playground on weekends. Yes, the entire train was painted blue, with a horizontal white stripe—perhaps representing a comet's tail—on the sides of the coaches. To reinforce the celestial illusion, each car on the train was given the name of an astronomer who had discovered an actual comet in the sky. It was a whimsical flight of fantasy in those wonderful years between the World Wars, with a destination that was like no other city on the planet.

The Lionel Standard gauge model here is even more colorful than the actual train, with its two-tone blue livery, ivory windows, and either brass or nickel trim. The locomotive, Lionel's finest steamer, has red wheels and a cowcatcher. The cars all have interior illumination and removable roofs to reveal the lavish details inside—hinged doors, swiveling seats, and washrooms with cathedral windows. The three cars bear the names of real-life astronomers Faye, Tempel, and Westphal.

Prized by collectors, the original *Blue Comet* outfits were introduced in 1930. They remained in the catalog until the Standard gauge era ended nine years later.

The *Transcontinental Limited*

Even the name of the *Transcontinental Limited* conjures up exciting images of a train speeding through the mountains and the prairies to the ocean, white with foam. This, the ultimate outfit in its day, is one of the biggest and most powerful and flamboyant trains Lionel has ever made. At an inch shy of nine feet long, it is huge, even for a Standard gauge set.

The electric-profile locomotive has twin super motors, two headlights, four running lights, operating pantographs, and a wealth of other added details.

The four passenger cars have two-bulb illumination and removable roofs to view the internal fittings—revolving seats, hinged doors, compartments, lavatories—plus a dome light and two red lantern lenses on the observation platform. Each car has a brass plate with the name of a state the train supposedly passed through: California, Colorado, Illinois, New York.

Collectors dubbed this masterpiece the "State Set." It came in two-tone brown or two-tone green and was cataloged as shown above from 1930 to 1933.

Standard gauge work train

"Work trains," also often known as "wreck trains" or "maintenance-of-way trains," were non-revenue-producing necessities used by the railroads to preserve the tracks and occasionally re-rail errant rolling stock.

Kids loved them for an obvious reason: train wrecks were common in the toy train world. Having a work train standing by gave added license to go ahead and derail the other train.

Lionel sold work trains in all gauges and price ranges over the years. The outfit pictured represents the top-of-the-line Standard gauge offering cataloged from 1931 to 1939.

The locomotive is the largest steamer the company ever made with distant-control reverse, headlight, running lights, built-in whistle, and red-glowing firebox.

The gondola is loaded with extra playtime features: four hollow wooden barrels that can be taken apart and a tin toolbox with four die-cast metal tools.

The crane car has a cab that swivels, a boom that can be raised and lowered, and a block and tackle with a big hook at the end of it.

The floodlight car has two movable light housings that can be switched on or off independently.

The stocky caboose features interior illumination along with a red rear platform light to mark the end of the train.

If this train set didn't keep a youngster quietly occupied for hours, it wasn't the fault of Lionel.

Union Pacific *M-10000* streamliner

Streamlined trains were big news in the early 1930s as America bootstrapped itself out of the Great Depression and looked forward optimistically to a bright future, underpinned by burgeoning technology, wherein everything would be bigger, better, easier, faster, and more glamorous. On the drawing boards of several American railroads were luxurious streamlined trains, pulled by shrouded steam locomotives or the new diesels. These futuristic trains were designed to cruise at more than 100 miles/hour while passengers cradled in air-conditioned comfort sipped beverages and watched the world whiz by.

The Union Pacific's articulated prototype, dubbed the *M-10000*, shattered a number of transcontinental speed records on its inaugural run and made a sensational appearance at Chicago's "Century of Progress" world's fair in February 1934. Undoubtedly, all the attendant publicity influenced the company's decision to model this trend-setting, permanently coupled train in O gauge.

Using a combination of die-cast and sheet-metal parts, this was the first venture Lionel made into producing a full scale model train. Because of the length of each car, a different track system with a wider turning radius had to be developed for it. Using a six-foot-diameter circle, the new O-72 gauge track paved the way for more scale models later.

The engineering department at Lionel had to work at top speed to develop this all-new train and track system and get it into production in a few short months. Once the *M-10000* was unveiled by the Union Pacific in February, Lionel had until the summer to get a picture for the catalog and until December to get the finished models into stores. Somehow, they did it.

The Union Pacific streamliner was cataloged from 1934 to 1941.

The *Hiawatha*

Named after Hiawatha, the Native American hero who could shoot an arrow and then outrun it, the Milwaukee Road's first streamlined train was all about speed. Sleek and luxurious inside and out, the all-new orange, maroon, and gray steam-powered train made its first run between Chicago and St. Paul at the end of May 1935, shaving 10 minutes off the existing record of 400 minutes set by a competing Chicago & North Western train.

The media frenzy began on day one with a buzz that was both loud and incessant. Apparently, dueling trains made news in those years between the World Wars. Boys idolized the *Hiawatha* engineers in the same way they would astronauts three decades later. One of the engineers even did an endorsement commercial for a breakfast cereal.

Again, as it had been the year before with the Union Pacific streamliner, the Lionel engineering department was under the gun. The *Hiawatha* train sets had to be designed, built, and shipped to stores in six months.

The O gauge locomotive was an almost exact scale model of the original. New high-pressure techniques were used for the first time to enhance even the smallest details on the completely die-cast metal locomotive body. The sheet-metal tender was equipped

with the new onboard air whistle.

Time was apparently running out when the decision was made to not build an entirely new passenger consist from scratch. Instead, designers modified the existing passenger cars designed for the Union Pacific streamliner to fit the *Hiawatha*. While not ideal, this decision allowed Lionel to meet the production deadline with another new top-of-the-line streamliner for 1935.

Both passenger and freight trains pulled by the *Hiawatha* locomotive were cataloged from 1935 to 1941. In 1942, only a freight train was offered.

Lionel reissued the passenger train from original tooling in 1988. To no one's surprise it was an overwhelming hit among toy train collectors.

The *Flying Yankee*

The battle of the streamliners was probably just as hot in the toy train world as it was in the real one. Lionel was ahead of the curve with its timely introduction of the Union Pacific *M-10000* in 1934 and, by 1935, had the Milwaukee Road's *Hiawatha* in development. But both of these were upscale products with a relatively limited sales potential during the Depression. So the company decided it also needed an authentic-looking streamlined train that was moderately priced to sell more broadly.

Amid a shower of publicity, Lionel's main competitor, American Flyer Manufacturing Company, had rushed to market with a cast-aluminum model of the Chicago, Burlington & Quincy's stainless-steel unitized *Zephyr* train the year before. In spite of a price tag that put it in the upper bracket, the *Zephyr* did reasonably well.

Lionel executives liked the concept and the appearance of the Budd-built *Zephyr* but didn't want to be put in the position of following Flyer's lead. Fortunately for them, the Boston & Maine had also purchased a Budd streamliner and had put it into service as the *Flying Yankee*. The trains were virtually identical except for the name.

Lionel came out with an O gauge model of the *Flying Yankee*. It fabricated the streamliner from chrome-plated sheet metal so American Flyer's aluminum *Zephyr* would look dull in comparison. To cement the sepulcher shut, the retail price Lionel set for the *Flying Yankee* was slightly less than half that of the *Zephyr*.

What happened next was a no-brainer. The *Flying Yankee* was cataloged from 1935 to 1941. The *Zephyr* went out of production in 1937.

O-27 Torpedo and Commodore Vanderbilt

The streamliner craze came on so fast in the 1930s that the major railroads had to scramble to keep abreast of it. As a stopgap, many of them had smooth shrouding put around existing steam locomotives on their prestige runs so they could be advertised as "streamlined" as well.

The Pennsylvania Railroad commissioned Raymond Loewy to design a bullet-nosed shroud for one of its class K4 Pacific 4-6-2 locomotives and used it on the *Broadway Limited* run between Chicago and New York. This engine was soon dubbed the "Torpedo."

Meanwhile, the New York Central had one of its Hudsons shrouded to pull the *Twentieth Century*

Limited between the same two cities. They named it the "Commodore Vanderbilt," after one of the railroad's founders.

By 1936, Lionel already had the *Hiawatha* and the Union Pacific at the top of the line and the *Flying Yankee* in the middle, so it decided to produce die-cast models of the Torpedo and the Commodore for its economy O-27 line.

Both engines caught on with toy train buyers on a budget who wanted to have streamliners running around their Christmas trees. The little Torpedo was particularly popular—it was in the catalog for six years.

Lionel mechanical handcars

These windup handcars made between 1934 and 1937 ran on track but weren't intended as part of the regular Lionel train line—they were too large for that. Instead, they might be classified as novelty toys.

The connection with Walt Disney is significant because Lionel was one of the first toymakers to obtain a license to produce replicas of his popular cartoon characters. The cars are stamped sheet metal, and the figures on them are made of molded composition.

Mickey Mouse Handcar. Mickey and Minnie bobbed up and down as they pumped the car. Appearing at Christmas 1934, it was not included in that season's catalog, but was listed the following three years.

Peter Rabbit Chick-Mobile. Peter pumped around the track with a basket of Easter eggs (missing in the photograph). Obviously, a springtime offering that wasn't very successful. Available as shown for use on track or as a floor toy, it was never in the catalog and was probably made for only one year, 1935.

Santa Claus Handcar. Santa shared his ride with a Christmas tree. Mickey Mouse's head could be seen popping out of Santa's removable backpack. This item was only made in 1935 and 1936.

Donald Duck Handcar. Cataloged in 1936 and 1937, this piece took handcar technology to the next level. A device inside the doghouse "quacked" in time with the movement of Donald's arms and Pluto's head.

All of these handcars are hard to find intact today because the composition figures were fragile. They are sought-after by Disney fans and toy collectors alike.

The Mickey Mouse circus outfit

The Mickey Mouse circus train of 1935 is colorful and packed with play value. The set includes a red windup locomotive with a headlight and a figure of Mickey himself shoveling coal from the tender, as well as three brightly lithographed trailers: dining car, band car, and animal car.

In addition, the set includes punch-out cardboard accessories to be assembled and placed within the oval of the track: a tent complete with a flying trapeze inside, a gas station, a commissary automobile, a billboard, a string of circus tickets, and a large molded replica of Mickey Mouse acting as a barker. A popular crowd-pleaser, this wonderful outfit promised hours of fun for children of all ages.

Today, this O-27 set is a highly desirable item for toy collectors, Disneyana buffs, and circus fans alike. Unfortunately, very few can still be found in good condition. The cardboard and molded composition parts were particularly vulnerable in the little hands that literally loved them to pieces.

Gift boxes of cars

So, Junior got a Lionel train for Christmas. Now what would he like for his birthday? Why, some more cars for it, of course!

This premise was behind one of the marketing strategies of the 1930s and early 1940s. Lionel sold set-extending gift packages of either freight or passenger cars of every series. That way, a young engineer's locomotive could do double duty and he would have a choice as to the kind of train he wanted

to run. If his train was a passenger, family members could buy him a set of freight cars to go with it. Or, relatives could get passenger cars if he had freights.

The four colorful O gauge freight cars that are shown here came in the gift packs of the mid-1930s. The three passenger cars were found in a similar O-27 package from 1942. For some reason, the gift packs did not return in the marketing programs that Lionel put together during the postwar years.

Grand Central

The most famous railroad station in the world was (and probably still is) New York City's Grand Central Terminal. This awe-inspiring stone structure—immortalized in story, song, and folklore, not to mention a few very popular radio programs and novels in the 1930s—was the inspiration for the largest and perhaps longest-running passenger station Lionel made (at right), cataloged from 1931 to 1949.

While the embossed-steel model was certainly not built to scale—that would have rivaled a sofa in size and overpowered everything else in a family's living room—it captured the essence and architectural style of the original and was massive enough to be used with either Standard or O gauge trains.

This grand station was replaced in the Lionel catalog by smaller, closer-to-scale replicas of the types of stations found in many moderately sized communities throughout the country.

The company's attempts at striking a happy medium with more universally familiar station configurations were undoubtedly successful. Still, they left much to be desired in the Glitz, Glory, and Glamour Department.

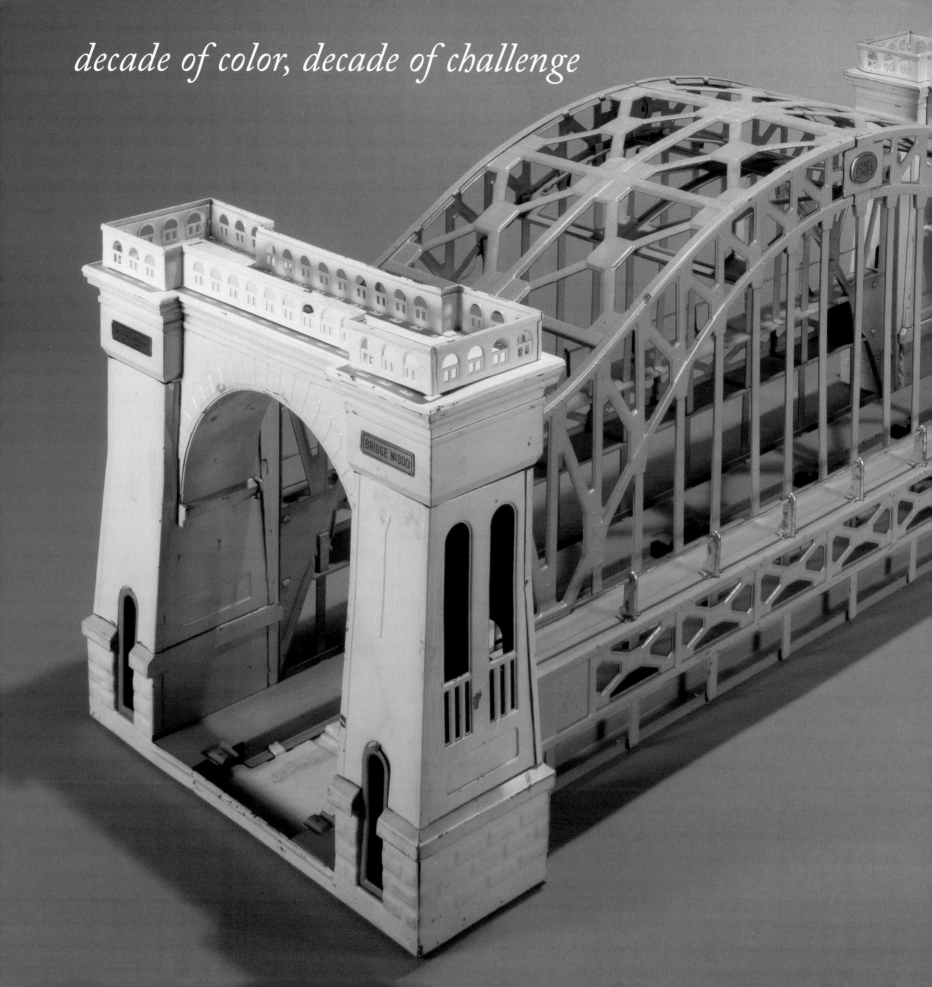

decade of color, decade of challenge

Hell Gate Bridge

Simple bridges were among the first accessories offered by Lionel. Most bridges required very little for installation other than a short run of straight track. They added much interest and realism to even the most basic train layouts.

The huge sheet-metal span shown here was a scaled-down model of New York's famous Hell Gate Bridge. Measuring 29 inches in length, it was intended for use with Standard gauge trains when first cataloged in 1928.

Because the Hell Gate Bridge remained in the Lionel catalog through 1942, a few years after the demise of Standard gauge, later illustrations showed this accessory with O gauge trains on it. Actually, the bridge looked more realistic when used with the smaller trains.

Golden Era

LIONEL TRAINS

When Americans want to depict a model train in advertising, art, or movies, they inevitably use one of two images: a smoking black steam locomotive or a racing red-and-silver Santa Fe diesel. Why? Because, thanks to the legendary trains from the golden era of Lionel, those two types of trains have become icons of American culture.

Lionel introduced its line of modern steamers first, starting in 1937. Using the then-new technology of high-pressure metal die-casting, it cataloged a line of new locomotives that were more detailed than those of the 1920s and early 1930s. When train production resumed following the Second World War, Lionel brought back into the line the best of its prewar trains, including the newer steam locomotives and operating accessories. But planners at Lionel had more than a few new items up their sleeves. One was a new type of realistic and easy-to-use "knuckle" coupler. Another was something so magical that the company kept it a closely guarded secret: smoke!

Company leaders also used new plastics to create locomotives and cars with better detail than ever before. Once production really got rolling, the company introduced new features and trains that still capture the imagination. From smoking, whistling locomotives to new diesels—including the dramatic Santa Fe—this was the Lionel line's golden era.

Lionel broadens its line

I n the 1930s, scale model railroading was not yet "the world's greatest hobby"—it was still very much in its infancy. The people involved had to be a combination of artist, machinist, and scrounger, and possess infinite patience and a lot of manual dexterity. Toy trains were either made by hand in home workshops or they were modified toys with details added to make them look more realistic. Imagination and craftsmanship were the keys, and O gauge ruled. Adults took this new spin on "playing with trains" very seriously.

Many of the homemade locomotives were on the crude side and didn't run very well. The few locomotive kits available required weeks of assembly time and often suffered from the same maladies. Contracting with a professional model maker was the only alternative. Such work was usually excellent, but that approach was not for everyone. A good custom-made locomotive could cost almost as much as a new Chevrolet.

Lionel watched this unfolding phenomenon very carefully and sensed a new market. If it could mass-produce a highly detailed scale model engine that ran well and was priced within reach of most hobbyists, the world would surely lay tracks to its door.

After two years of preparation, in 1937 Lionel unveiled its masterpiece: an exact 1:48 scale replica of the popular New York Central Hudson-type 4-6-4 steam locomotive. The model was superb and accurate down to the smallest detail. It ran like a champ because of special gearing that allowed for realistically slow speeds. All the experimentation Lionel made with precision, high-pressure metal die-casting culminated in this one museum-quality gem. There was even a new solid T-rail track system designed for it.

The scale Hudson was sold separately with its own walnut-finished display stand in a passenger outfit appropriately called the *Rail Chief*.

A less-detailed "semi-scale" version of the locomotive, which ran on tubular track and coupled with regulation Lionel freight and passenger cars, was also available in high-end toy train outfits. By all indications, this stripped-down rendition far outsold the full-scale model. Of course, its price was quite a bit lower and its potential customers of those involved with toy trains outnumbered scale model railroaders in those days. Still, Lionel took this as a strong indication that all of its customers wanted scale-like realism in their electric trains. That would be the next general trend.

In 1938 five new "super-detailed" die-cast metal steam locomotives were offered on all price levels—four of them resembled the Hudson. Only three sheet-metal steam locomotives remained in the catalog.

The 1939 line featured scale and semi-scale models of a Pennsylvania Railroad 0-6-0 switch engine to go with the Hudsons. Another die-cast metal steamer entered the roundhouse. Many of the smaller locomotives that had been painted gunmetal gray were changed to flat black.

For 1940, all colors were dulled down and reverted to earth tones and more railroad-like shades. The bright number boards disappeared, replaced by rubber-stamped lettering. Lionel began experimenting with a phenolic plastic named Bakelite for use in car bodies. Four new scale and semi-scale freight cars—a die-cast metal caboose, hopper, tank car, and a Bakelite boxcar—joined the lineup, along with a smaller switch engine for lower-priced sets. A special two-train set that featured "Magic-Electrol," an independent locomotive control, appeared for the first time. Two trains on the same track—how much more realistic could running toy trains become? "Scale" and "realism" were stressed in the 1940 catalog, along with a classic photo of a boy measuring his locomotives with a ruler and saying "dead ringers for the big fellows."

The 1941 catalog continued the realism theme, with many close-up pictures of details on locomotives and cars. Colors became even more muted and flat, with emphasis on Tuscan red and black. Three "scale-detailed" sheet-metal freight cars—a four-door automobile boxcar, tanker, and Pennsylvania caboose—and a Pullman with a Bakelite body were added. They had a scale look but were a bit smaller than the full-scale cars. Coal tenders replaced other types in almost all sets. By this time, Lionel was devoting some of its production capacity to military contracts so, to compensate and make the line seem as though it had more new items than it actually did, different car series were mixed together in some sets. The technique proved very effective.

In 1942, there were even more odd mixes and shortfalls because of the wartime ban on non-essential manufacturing that took effect in July. Because toy trains were made from materials critical to the war effort, their production was banned for the duration. The scale Hudson had been on the catalog cover every year since it was introduced. For 1942, designers at Lionel posed it in front of an American flag.

Streamliners remained popular throughout the period. There was the Union Pacific *M-10000* and the *Hiawatha* in O-72. The *Flying Yankee* and the *City of Denver* in O gauge were joined by an unnamed streamliner that vaguely resembled several prototypes in O-27. The Pennsylvania Torpedo and the New York Central Commodore Vanderbilt locomotives came in two sizes: one for O gauge, the other for O-27.

The 1938 introduction by Lionel of remote-control,

1940

THAT'S THE SCALE MODEL FOR US, SON!

Kids loved the couplers and didn't mind assisting them by hand once in a while.

Once the remote-control couplers were established, it wasn't a far stretch to introduce a series of automatic operating cars, using the same basic technology. An unloading button appeared next to the uncoupling button on the control for the new remote-control track sections. The coal dump cars came first, in 1938. The next year, automatic log, barrel, and merchandise cars were added. So, within the space of less than a decade, Lionel trains reversed, whistled, uncoupled, and unloaded—all by remote control.

Accessories also got bigger and more functional, adding to the play value and providing little slice-of-life vignettes drawn from industrial America. In rapid succession between 1938 and 1940, there appeared a coal elevator, log loader, magnet crane, and bascule bridge. They were all motorized and swung into action at the touch of a button.

In terms of the number of different outfits in the catalog, 1940 and 1941 were the company's biggest prewar years, with 42 outfits in O, O-27, and O-72 gauges both years. By stark contrast, there were only 16 sets in the 1942 catalog because of the government ban—and some of them may not

electromagnetic automatic couplers created a sensation and a permanent, sweeping change in toy train technology. They presented another element of realism and control. Operators could automatically couple and uncouple cars and put together and break apart trains without touching them. It could be done only at points where special remote-control tracks were installed, but that hardly mattered.

Automatic box couplers were an instant success. Designed to be compatible with existing manual latch couplers, the new couplers from the start had some shortcomings—they didn't always couple when they should or uncouple where they should. Several modifications later, these flaws were minimized, but they never went away.

actually have been made. Standard Gauge was a thing of the past, and the fledgling OO gauge, produced from 1938 to 1942, never found a viable market.

One of the most interesting observations regarding this period was the rise of O-27 to the important position it would hold in the Lionel hierarchy for many years to come.

Even though there were no electric trains, Lionel prospered during the Second World War. The company turned out precision navigational equipment for the U. S. Navy and Merchant Marine and instruments for the Army Air Corps.

For 1943, Lionel offered a "wartime train kit" in the size and shape of a conventional Lionel freight train but made of "non-essential" materials—lithographed cardstock and wood. The venture was a disaster. The kit was too complicated for a child to assemble without help and the finished train kept falling apart. Only the ads continued in 1944 and 1945.

When the war ended in August 1945, Lionel had a mere three months to get some kind of train merchandise into the stores. The very limited line that year featured only one train outfit and an assortment of accessories, probably put together from leftover inventory of prewar parts. The train had a popular steam locomotive and three scale-detailed cars. In this set there was one new car: a gondola intended for 1942 that had been put on hold.

The big news for 1945 concerned the new remote-control real-railroad knuckle couplers on the train. Lionel had used the three-year hiatus in production to take a revolutionary step in its coupler design—something the

company had been contemplating for years but put off because it didn't want to make the existing box couplers obsolete overnight. With some upgrading, the new couplers would become the industry standard. All the toy train manufacturers today use their own versions of them.

With the long war finally over and peacetime production reinstated all across America, the light was green. The track was clear for Lionel to lead the way into what became the Golden Age of Toy Trains.

The scale Hudson

The crowning achievement of all time at Lionel has to be the exact 1:48 scale model of a New York Central Hudson 4-6-4 steam locomotive it introduced in 1937. Of museum quality and accuracy, this masterpiece of model making was also very functional. It targeted operators of O scale model railroads, but appealed to everyone who saw it. New York Central president Frank Williamson kept one on his mantelpiece and vouched for the model's authenticity.

It took two years just to produce the dies and tooling for the scale Hudson. Assembly of each model was highly labor-intensive, taking some 30 minutes to complete and test.

The Hudson model was accurate down to the smallest item—every cylinder, piping, pop valve, hand-rail, rivet, bolt, and nut. It featured a movable bell, open spoke wheels, fully operating valve gear,

and a front drop coupler with its lift pin that actually worked. The word "Timken"" was visible on the roller-bearing truck caps. Lionel boasted that the tender had "1,600 rivets, just like the real thing." The model was designed to run only on the new Lionel solid T-rail track but could be adapted for layouts that used an outside third rail.

At the same time, Lionel brought out what it called a "semi-scale" version of the Hudson. This considerably less-detailed model was outfitted to run on regular tinplate track. It sold quite well among the upscale train buyers who didn't operate scale model railroads. It was this semi-scale Hudson that was reissued in the postwar period and a number of times in recent years.

The original full-scale Hudson was last offered for sale in 1942. By that time, the demand for O scale models was dwindling as model railroad builders

looked toward HO and the
other smaller scales that took up
less space.

   Joseph L. Bonanno, who headed the
Lionel engineering department when the Hudson
was in development, summarized the saga well: "This
locomotive represents Lionel's greatest achievement in
designing, tooling, and mass producing a scale model
of one of the most popular locomotives of the time,
at a fraction of the cost of handmade models. I doubt
whether any model made for mass production will ever
compare in quality and workmanship...."

Semi-scale Hudson outfit

When Lionel entered the exact scale arena, trying to attract serious model railroaders as well as toy train buyers with a line that covered the entire O gauge spectrum, it proceeded slowly and with deliberate caution. The Union Pacific and *Hiawatha* streamliners came first in 1934 and 1935. The Hudson arrived in 1937. A model of an 0-6-0 switch engine appeared in 1939. Scale freight cars for the Hudson and the switcher weren't made until 1940.

Obviously, Lionel must have been developing a long-range plan toward scale-ization that was interrupted by the Second World War and later curtailed. Company leaders eventually scrapped this plan because the O scale market seemed to be drying up.

Some unusual pairings took place in the transition. The scale Hudson outfit had four modified

Hiawatha cars painted two-tone red for the first three years. A freight consist was added in 1940. Likewise, the 0-6-0 switcher didn't have a scale train its first year.

Meanwhile, planners at Lionel decided that "semi-scale" versions of these two locomotives—less detailed and equipped to be compatible with the firm's regular electric train line—should be put up in sets for the general train market.

This 1938 outfit is a classic example. It is headed by a new die-cast metal semi-scale Hudson, painted gunmetal gray to differentiate it from the black scale locomotives. Everything behind it, including the Vanderbilt oil tender, comes from the high end of the regular sheet-metal toy train line and had been in production for between four and a dozen years at the time.

The Lionel philosophy of cautious evolution rather than revolution is certainly evident here. This beautiful and colorful transition O-72 gauge outfit bears testimony to how the company made it work. Somehow, the inherent incongruities leave this train all the more charming and compelling.

The Lionel "scale-detailed" line

This wasn't a cataloged outfit as such, but we put it together to show the excellent realism that Lionel even managed to incorporate into its middle-price-range locomotives and cars immediately before the Second World War.

The locomotive, which follows no particular prototype, has the heft and brawny look of many major railroad steamers of the day. All the little details down to the rivet heads are sharply visible on the boiler casting. The hinged boiler front with a convex headlight lens that actually casts a beam and the added handrail supports, piping, bell, pop valves, and dummy whistle are the same as those used on the scale Hudson. The latest Baldwin disc-style driving wheels were state-of-the-art then. The realistically cast and detailed tender holds the Lionel patented built-in air whistle sound effect.

The three all-metal freight cars are from the scale-detailed line introduced in 1941. The Pennsylvania Railroad automobile boxcar has four sliding doors, steps, and ladders. The Sunoco tanker sports a wealth of added details such as ladders, handrails, a brake wheel, and destination markers. The caboose, the latest Pennsy type, has interior illumination through diffused window panels. The cars all have brake cylinders and underbody details previously found on only the most deluxe Lionel models.

That was the direction Lionel's middle-of-the-road trains were taking when the war hit. The freight cars, painted somewhat differently, survived into the early postwar period until they were replaced by cheaper plastic models. The locomotive dies were modified significantly, and this model re-emerged in 1947 with a smoke unit and a radically altered appearance. As such, it ran for another six years.

Bascule bridge

Of all the dozens of different bridges Lionel has manufactured during its long history, the bascule bridge is the one that young railroaders have wanted most. This operating accessory is a masterpiece from the late prewar era, a time of production still celebrated for its automated marvels of toy train engineering.

The bascule bridge has a very realistic structure and appearance, down to the little bridge tender's house. It works like many of the counterbalanced drawbridges that could once be seen all over the country.

The fascinating action cycle begins at the touch of a button. The bridge lifts slowly and noisily until it reaches its zenith, pauses a moment, then deliberately descends to the horizontal position. Power to the track on both ends is automatically cut off to avoid accidents while the bridge is up. Of course, there is a red light on top of the thing.

One of the larger Lionel accessories, the bascule bridge requires quite a bit of space and trackage to work believably, so it isn't often found on small layouts. It was cataloged for seven years between 1940 and 1949 and reissued 50 years later as part of the Lionel centennial.

Passenger sets of the streamlined era

Americans were brimming with confidence at the end of the Second World War, and America's railroads were no exception. They shouldered astonishing burdens during the war without faltering. Whether taking mountains of coal from the mines of Appalachia to power plants and factories in the Great Plains states, rivers of steel from the mills of Gary and Pittsburgh to the factories of Detroit, or oceans of grain from the Midwest to both coasts, they got the job done—and done well.

The same had been true on the passenger side. Passenger traffic had dropped through the 1930s as both the Great Depression and the growth of a national highway system cut into their traditional markets. But during the war the number of passengers—and the number of miles they traveled—soared. From limiteds to locals, mail trains to troop trains, nearly every train ran full and then some. The railroads were betting that if they could

introduce new streamliners to replace their older equipment, they could keep their trains running full. Their biggest problem, however, was they would not have their new equipment in service nearly as soon as they wanted due to the huge backlog of orders at the passenger car manufacturers and the postwar shortages of materials. Railroads, therefore, had to try to satisfy customers with older equipment, at least temporarily.

The situation was much the same on the Lionel Lines. The prewar passenger lineup included stamped-metal models of standard "heavyweight" passenger

equipment, stamped-metal articulated streamliners, and the scale-detailed *Irvington* heavyweights which were molded in tough, durable Bakelite plastic. None of the cars, however, bore more than a passing resemblance to the streamliners that the railroads were operating—or at least publicizing.

Thus Lionel also needed a new line of passenger equipment if it hoped to keep its customers happy. However, getting that line into service would take time because even Lionel could not design and tool an entire new line in just a year or two. A product line without passenger trains was unthinkable, so the older equipment would have to serve for a few more years.

The first passenger cars after the war came in 1946. The small metal coaches reappeared in several different sets, all powered by steam locomotives. No new passenger-style trucks were available, so these cars had to ride on freight trucks. They were delightfully colorful and even a bit nostalgic, but they weren't streamliners.

Neither were the top-of-the-line cars of that era, the *Irvington* heavyweights. Other than their couplers, these cars were the same as those produced before the war. Realistic (and drab) they were; modern they weren't.

The outfits the heavyweights came in were wonderful, though. Some had the exciting new Pennsylvania "Turbine" (so dubbed because it was a model of an experimental steam-turbine locomotive) as their power, and others had the powerful, detailed Berkshire. Still others included the new-for-1947 GG1 electric, a streamlined 20-wheeled beauty built in the prewar style with all metal parts. (Like most of the early postwar Lionel trains, the GG1s strengthened the forearms of

many a young engineer!) And a lucky few had the 1950 version of the Hudson at the head of their passenger outfits, this time with smoke, Magne-Traction, and a whistle. Wow!

The first new Lionel postwar passenger cars had arrived two years before, in 1948. Though far from being scale size (they were detailed models), their appearance suggests that Lionel product planners were hedging their bets a bit. The cars have the arched roofs and blunt ends of streamlined cars and the observation car has a rounded end rather than a platform, but the cars also have the rivets characteristic of heavyweight cars. (A few lightweight streamlined cars did have rivets, but most had either completely smooth sides or corrugated stainless steel panels.)

Moreover, these new passenger cars were not painted silver, or even the two-tone gray the Pullman Company used for most of its sleepers during the postwar era. Instead, the first of these cars wore a traditional green with yellow trim. (In 1950 they wore a vibrant yellow and in succeeding years they

were silver, sometimes with gray, blue, or red trim. They remained in the line through the mid-1960s and reappeared 10 years after that.). These cars looked great with the Turbine and other steam locomotives, though, and they allowed Lionel to retire the old sheet-metal coaches after 1949.

By 1950, the streamlined era was in full bloom on the real railroads and the traditionally cutting-edge Lionel Lines was behind the power curve. The company needed new cars but, with the Korean War at its hottest, that was not possible.

However, by 1952 Lionel had cars so dramatic, so striking, and so realistic that they leapt to the top of the catalog. What were these cars? A set of illuminated aluminum streamliners, including (depending on the outfit and the year) a baggage car, a Pullman sleeper, a round-end observation car, and that icon of the postwar era, a dome car.

United with a pair of gleaming Santa Fe diesels, the new streamliners made an unforgettable set—one that raced around the living rooms and train rooms of America with

By this point the GG1s had two Magne-Traction motors and the same horn as the diesels. Early GG1s had one motor without Magne-Traction and a rattling buzzer for a horn. Magne-Traction, a system involving magnets mounted in the frame, wheels, and (sometimes) axles, caused locomotives to grip rails with greater force than their weight alone would allow. Lionel followed the Pennsy's lead by painting the GG1 Tuscan red.

What a locomotive! It was strong, smooth, and boasted a resonant, powerful sound that even the F3 didn't have. The passenger cars wore narrow Tuscan and gold stripes like the real train. Today, *Congressional* outfits remain treasured.

nearly the same grandeur and grace of the real *Super Chief* or *California Zephyr*. The first set came with two Pullmans, a dome, and an observation. It was Lionel at its peak—the finest outfit of the top sales year in the company's golden era.

The aluminum streamliners may never have duplicated the impact they made in their first year, but other equally legendary sets followed. Over the next few years, Lionel offered those cars with the company's small Hudson, burly Train Master diesel, and assorted F3 diesels, including the Canadian Pacifics of 1957. In 1958 Lionel used the name *Super Chief* to describe the Santa Fe streamliner, back for a return engagement (and wearing zippy red stripes from 1959 to 1961).

Lionel didn't forget its fans in the East when it planned its streamliner outfits, though. It offered the cars with two electric-profile locomotives: the snappy EP-5 and the majestic GG1. The former made for a neat set, but the latter sets—offered in 1955 and 1956 and called *Congressional* after the Pennsylvania Railroad train—were true classics.

The last Lionel streamliners of the golden era came in the early 1960s in the form of the "Presidential" cars. With Dwight Eisenhower leaving office and John Kennedy coming in, interest in the presidency was high. Lionel marketers thought that a set of cars named for chief executives would compete well with the new space toys and slot cars.

The streamliners looked nice with gold striping and black lettering, but Lionel made what still seems a curious choice when it named them for Presidents McKinley, Garfield, and Harrison. Offered with both the GG1 and the Santa Fe F3, they made for attractive, if somewhat odd, outfits.

While we're on the subject of presidents, Ike's popularity may have combined with the late-1950s Civil War boom to motivate Lionel to introduce its other passenger train of the era: the 1860s-themed *General* sets. These nostalgia-oriented outfits ran from 1959 through 1962 in various permutations. Given that they appeared in the same catalogs as Lionel space cars, streamliners,

and conventional freight outfits, though, it seems clear that they were another sign of the firm's confusion during the era.

By the mid-1950s, of course, America's full-scale railroads had recognized that passenger traffic was dropping, and fast. Some lines tried to cut costs while maintaining quality service by purchasing self-propelled (via a small diesel) coaches called Rail Diesel Cars. Lionel introduced its own RDCs in 1956, also based on the mechanism from its diesels. They were nicely detailed, but never big sellers.

The biggest challenge that Lionel passenger trains faced, though, probably wasn't space toys or slot cars. It was the company's own freight outfits. Passenger sets were beautiful, but aside from racing from depot to depot, what could you do with them? But a Lionel freight could do it all. As we'll see, Lionel offered nearly every type of freight car that the real railroads had, plus a few that they didn't.

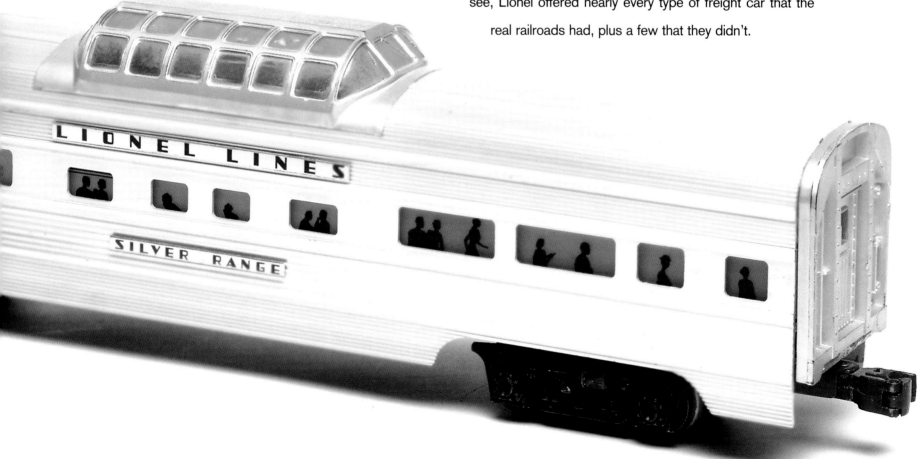

The Santa Fe

Bulky black steam locomotives were the image of the toy train in the late 1940s. With their flailing rods and echoing whistles, these rugged, smoke-puffing powerhouses highballed freight and passenger trains across the pages of the Lionel catalog and through the living rooms and basements of America. Fascinating and powerful though they were, however, they were most definitely not colorful.

Toy train locomotives had not always been so drab, of course. The trains of the 1920s and 1930s had been a riot of color. After the Second World War, however, the toy train manufacturers offered realistic, but dull, workhorses—until 1948, that is.

That was the year Lionel introduced its General Motors F3. The New York Central and the Santa Fe had each paid part of the cost of developing the model, so it was available in either paint scheme. However, the Santa Fe version was the star, both then and now.

Where the New York Central model came in that road's elegant two-tone gray, the Santa Fe version wore the unforgettable "warbonnet" red-and-silver design.

Quite simply, the Santa Fe F3 became America's favorite toy train. Lionel made them by the thousands. Entertainers mentioned them on the radio, ballplayers and movie stars ran them on their own layouts, and American boys all across the country went to sleep with

LIONEL *Triple Unit* DIESELS
Equipped with REALISTIC HORN and *MAGNE-TRACTION*

Now, for the first time, Lionel offers a train set featuring a triple unit Diesel locomotive. Here is freight hauling in its most modern form. The Lionel GM-type Diesel is the giant of the model railroading field — equipped with two motors and *Magne-Traction* — capable of handling just about any power, speed or performance test you want to give it.

THE LAST WORD IN FREIGHT HAULING—LIONEL Nos. 2191W AND 2193W 4-CAR DIESEL FREIGHTS

Picture yourself at the throttle of one of these big "growlers," streaking across the plains, over the mountains, delivering a full load of freight to destination. From pilot coupler to the rear end of the "shanty" this is honest-to-goodness railroading all the way. Triple unit Diesel itself measures almost 40 inches long! Your freight includes that minutely-scaled gondola with barrels, the stock car for your cattle shippers, the Lehigh Valley hopper car and an illuminated caboose. Your choice of a big Eastern or Western railway ... specify by number ... the 2191W is the Santa Fe, the 2193W is the New York Central. These freights are 6 ft., 4 ins. long. Track forms oval 70½" x 31½".

Lionel Sets No. 2191W Santa Fe and No. 2193W New York Central Comprise:
1 No. 2343 Santa Fe or 2344 N.Y. Central Twin Diesel, both with Magne-Traction
1 No. 2343C Santa Fe or 2344C New York Central "B" Unit
1 No. 6462 Gondola Car
1 No. 6656 Stock Car
1 No. 6456 Lehigh Valley R.R. Hopper Car
1 No. 6457 Illuminated Caboose
8 sec. OC Curved Track
7 sec. OS Straight Track
1 UCS Remote Control Track Set
CTC Lockon, Lubricant, Instruction Booklet

PRICE FOR EITHER SET
$70.00

thoughts of them in their heads. Did they dare hope to get a Santa Fe from Santa Claus? For thousands, the dream came true.

The Lionel Santa Fe F3 became the most famous and most loved electric train ever produced; even today it's one of the indelible images of the holiday season. Indeed, the Santa Fe has become a part of American culture. That staying power is due in no small measure to the brilliant ways Lionel associated the image of the Santa Fe with the holidays in its catalogs and advertising.

For the boys and girls who had them, though, the Santa Fe was simply the neatest, nicest toy they ever had. Lionel made sure that every Santa Fe F3, whatever the version, had a top-quality motor (usually two), a horn, and plenty of detail. They were built so well that 50-year-old Santa Fes still burnish the rails of layouts across America.

As Lionel begins its second century, it continues to introduce new models and innovations. Among them is a new Santa Fe, the company's finest ever. There's still plenty of life in this legend.

1950 Hudson passenger set

After an eight-year absence, the semi-scale Hudson locomotive reappeared for Lionel's golden anniversary in 1950. It had been modified to negotiate regular 31-inch-diameter O gauge curves with ease and upgraded with a smoke unit and Magne-Traction.

The signature outfit coupled the Hudson with three of Lionel's finest Tuscan-colored, scale-detailed, heavy-weight Pullman cars, named *Madison*, *Manhattan*, and *Irvington*, which had also been spruced up for the occasion with silhouettes of passengers in the windows. Undoubtedly, this was the greatest train Lionel had offered to date in those postwar years.

Apparently, sales were not as brisk as Lionel had anticipated because the mighty Hudson was discontinued after only one season. It would take 14 more years for the Hudson to come back. The Pullman cars never did return (at least not until the special commemorative Lionel centennial trains five decades later). They were soon to be replaced in the mainstream by streamlined, extruded aluminum passenger cars. Clearly, an era had ended.

Fortunately, the semi-scale Hudson returned, first in the mid-1960s for a three-year run, then again in the mid-1980s. The full-scale model was reissued in 1990.

The greatest of the great

Streamliner! Even the name had a magical quality during Lionel's golden era. Only a generation before, America's passenger limiteds had "heavyweight" steel cars. These cars were as stout as battleships but their styling was industrial (at best!) and they were hot in the summer (and often cold in the winter).

But the new passenger cars of the 1940s and 1950s were different, inside and out. With air conditioning, comfortable seats in the coaches, individual rooms in the Pullman-operated sleepers, and big "picture" windows, they were a delight to ride, sturdy yet lovely. Some cars carried the colors of their owners but many were made of shimmering stainless steel.

Lionel streamlined outfits made their first appearance in the 1952 catalog and were nearly as glamorous as the trains they were modeled after. Although Lionel would manufacture several other streamlined sets during its golden era (and dozens more in the 1980s and 1990s), none was more exciting than the first.

Known as the *Super Speedliner*, this four-car train included everything that made the Lionel trains of the 1950s great. The first F3 diesels had the early-style motors unmatched for durability or pulling power, plus Magne-Traction and a horn. They also had the widest array of add-on details of any Lionel diesel of the era and wore the Santa Fe's unforgettable red-and-silver paint scheme.

The four streamlined passenger cars featured extruded aluminum bodies that were tough enough to survive a high-speed derailment and still look good. They also included highly detailed cast trucks and ends and were, in a word, magnificent.

The set included enough rugged O gauge track to let the train stretch out a bit (though dealers were always happy to sell additional sections of track), but no transformer. (Very few O gauge sets included one, perhaps because Lionel surmised that many buyers of these higher-priced outfits already owned a transformer.) It's a safe bet, though, that most Lionel railroaders used a powerful KW or ZW transformer to make sure their Santa Fes could reach top speed.

The greatest Lionel O gauge set ever? That's a tough call—so many have become legends—but it's difficult to imagine any other single outfit that has had the impact of this one. You know what? On second thought, we'll say yes.

Golden anniversary passenger set

In 1950, Lionel celebrated its 50th anniversary in business in a big way. New outfits and rolling stock were introduced with a flourish. A few old favorites, such as the semi-scale Hudson steam locomotive returned. Magne-Traction, a system devised to improve the pulling power of toy train locomotives, was unveiled with an oversized fanfare.

Probably the most endearing 1950 offering of all was the colorful Union Pacific streamliner in the moderately priced O-27 line. Its golden-yellow, red, and gray paint scheme appeared in the catalog on only one passenger outfit in only one year, Lionel's golden jubilee.

Although Lionel prosaically referred to it as a "sleek, diesel, three-Pullman set," this train has subsequently captured the fancy of collectors, who usually call it the "50th anniversary set."

The rather stubby back-to-back diesel locomotives

modeled after the American Locomotive Company's FA cab units were new that year. Even though they have since appeared in dozens of liveries and logos, the 1950 Union Pacifics are the ones toy train fans most cherish.

The three streamlined passenger cars were not new, having been introduced in green two years before, but they sported a new color scheme and new names: *Plainfield*, *Westfield*, and *Livingston*, following the Lionel pattern of naming cars in this series after New Jersey towns. The real Union Pacific railroad didn't run anywhere near New Jersey at the time and tended to name its cars after western locations, but that didn't seem to matter. Lionelville was a very forgiving place.

The yellow UP Alcos were also packed with a four-car freight outfit in 1950. The next year, Lionel changed the color to an aluminum shade on the locomotives and the passenger cars.

The mighty GG1

During the Golden Era of the postwar period, Lionel trains were the dream of boys (and girls) across the nation. But the heart of Lionel country was undoubtedly the East Coast. This was the wealthiest and most densely populated part of the country and the region in which the company itself made its home.

The king of the Eastern roads was the mighty Pennsylvania, the "Standard Railroad of the World." The expresses on its electrified main line between New York and Washington carried the captains of American commerce and the leaders of the republic. And the locomotive that pulled these expresses was the mighty GG1 electric.

Introduced in 1947, the O gauge model of a GG1 is more than worthy of the name "Lionel." Although its die-cast metal body was slightly shortened to fit on Lionel curves, it nonetheless captures the real GG1's distinctive shape. Its add-on details and complex running gear add to the impressions of speed and power that the model creates. It was—and is—a beauty.

Through 1949, Lionel GG1s had one motor with a design similar to that of the motor used to power the Turbine and Berkshire. In 1950, Lionel introduced a two-motored GG1 with Magne-Traction. More powerful than the original, it could pull nearly any train a Lionel engineer put behind it and would look great doing so.

The *General* set

As the centennial of the Civil War approached, the three major toy train manufacturers—American Flyer, Lionel, and Marx—came up with 1860s-era sets to capitalize on all the attention that period in American history would soon draw.

The Lionel model was based upon the *General*, a woodburning 4-4-0 locomotive that actually saw wartime service on the Western & Atlantic Railroad.

Three new cars were designed to go with the locomotive and tender: an official U.S. Mail car, a passenger coach, and a horse corral—essentially a flatcar with a fence around it and six or seven plastic horses (the catalog says six, but the example we photographed had seven). The cars all authentically represented the wooden construction of prototypes from the middle of the 19th century.

This very appealing and colorful train appeared in Lionel catalogs from 1959 to 1962. All the components have been reissued several times in different liveries since, beginning in the late 1970s.

The hard-working heroes of Lionel

Just as Joshua Lionel Cowen's first freight car launched the Lionel empire, it was freight locomotives, cars, and outfits that carried the line to new heights during its golden postwar years.

When the Second World War ended, not only was the only Lionel outfit for 1945 a freight set, but the first all-new item of any kind was the Pennsylvania Railroad gondola that came with it. The 1946 catalog listed 23 outfits, but only 8 were passenger sets. From then on, the balance in the catalog (and on the Lionel sales ledger) would always favor freights.

Given the number of loads a freight could carry, it was more fun than a passenger outfit. Freight cars cost less for Lionel to make, so freight sets could carry lower prices or include more items for a given price.

Freights also allowed Lionel to include cars from multiple railroads in a set, widening the set's geographic appeal. It

wasn't by accident that virtually all Lionel steam locomotives of this era bore the name "Lionel Lines" on their tenders, or that their trains included cars from such railroads as the Santa Fe, Southern Pacific, Erie, New York Central, and Pennsy. With a "Lionel Lines" locomotive, an Eastern car, and a Western car, the outfit would sell in nearly any city from Boston to San Diego, and the lucky young recipient would have at least one car that was, "just like the one I saw last week, Dad, honest!"

Lionel introduced its first family of new freight cars right after the war, starting in 1945 and continuing through 1946 and

1947. It included a plastic-bodied boxcar, stockcar, gondola, tank car, hopper car, refrigerator car, and (in 1948) caboose. Also new were several cars that were mostly made from die-cast metal: operating log and ore cars, a crane, a flatcar that could also form the base for a work-train caboose, and a depressed-center flatcar for heavy loads. The cars were slightly smaller than the prewar scale-detailed cars in size, but they were nicely detailed and wore realistically drab colors.

Also new were several steam locomotives, including the Turbine, Berkshire, and K4 Pacific, plus some revised versions of the newer prewar steamers. Most of these were modeled on locomotives that were primarily freight haulers or pinch-hit on freights.

Like the freight cars, these Lionel steamers were all slightly smaller than scale, but most had a substantial number of separate details and each had a top-quality motor. The GG1 electric had the same motor as the Turbine and Berkshire plus a heavy die-cast metal body. Most steamers also came with whistle tenders (or, on the GG1, a buzzing "horn"), and the larger steam locomotives came with the toy train hit of the era—real puffing smoke.

Smoke had been an unreachable dream for model railroaders and model train manufacturers for many years, but the means of achieving it (cotton? lit cigarettes?) eluded them. The Lionel engineering team actually developed two methods for making smoke for postwar use. The first, employed only in 1946, used a large light bulb to melt tablets of ammonium nitrate. These steamers smoked well enough, but Lionel dropped this method because the resulting vapor corroded the locomotives.

On most steam locomotives from 1947 and later, a small wire heating element in a cylinder (picture a tiny toaster inside a short pill bottle) heated a tablet made from a wax that smoked when heated. It was a big hit.

By 1948, Lionel had introduced the F3 diesels (another type that hauled both freight and passenger trains). By 1950, the General Motors NW2 diesel switcher and Alco FA diesels had joined the roster.

Now product planners at Lionel had roughly ten locomotives and a dozen major freight car types from which to choose. That selection allowed them to create a nearly endless variety of freight sets. Each new catalog brought at least a few new outfits, some with entirely new combinations of cars and others with only a few changes.

During these years operating freight cars became overwhelming favorites of young Lionel railroaders. Cars that dumped logs or coal and searchlight cars had existed before the war, as had boxcars that ejected simulated boxes at alarming velocities. (It was a good thing that few fragile items traveled the Lionel Lines. Between the speeds at which the line's young engineers took the curves and the

vigor with which the solenoid-powered operating cars emptied their loads, the resulting damage claims would have broken the bank!) Lionel quickly introduced similar cars in the new line of freight cars, and both products were very robust.

It was the two newest operating cars, however, that became the real stars of the line and remain legends today. The first was the famous milk car, basically a newly designed refrigerator carbody with a mechanism inside that delivered small metal "milk cans" onto a trackside platform. A figure was placed on the arm of the mechanism, making it appear that a (very, very cold!) miniature man lived in the car and delivered the cans. The other was the cattle car, which used a vibrating mechanism to make miniature cattle "walk" through a pen. Each was an absolute hit.

This group of locomotives and cars formed the entire Lionel line until the mid-1950s. Then came an explosion of color and creativity that echoes to this day. Indeed, some of the actual cars developed during the period remained available into the late 1990s.

It was during these years that America's railroads, no longer plagued with clouds of dirty coal smoke thanks to the new diesels, reintroduced bright colors to their freight cars. So did Lionel, whose new cars were larger (to go with the newer, larger diesels), more colorful, and simpler to assemble. Once again Lionel developed a boxcar, stockcar, flatcar, tank car, refrigerator car, and all the other types found on the real railroads.

Lionel didn't stop there, however. In the search for items that would compete more effectively with the

space toys, cowboy toys, and other distractions of the late 1950s, designers created models that reflected the new types of cars appearing on American railroads, such as double-deck automobile cars, generator cars, and bay-window cabooses. Then they created a variety of cars that were uncommon, to say the least. How about an aquarium car with "swimming" fish? Or a giant, 16-wheel flat that carried girders? Other cars carried railroad wheels, piggyback trailers, firefighting equipment, and pickles in giant barrels.

As new locomotive types appeared on the railroads, they appeared on the Lionel Lines. Railroads were ordering boxy "road switcher" diesels by the thousands during this period because these versatile locomotives could haul expresses and freights or switch in a freight

yard. Lionel followed suit with its Fairbanks-Morse Train Master, a twin-motored, scale-sized behemoth that dwarfed nearly every other Lionel locomotive. Next came a model of the General Motors GP7 diesel, which was also the first Lionel diesel to have a stamped rather than a die-cast metal frame.

Oddly, though, these detailed locomotives appeared in the catalog at the same time as a group of the most fanciful Lionel cars. A gondola with a miniature cop chasing a hobo and a boxcar with a miniature brakeman who fell flat when approaching low clearances were among the more realistic of these cars. Stockcars with ducking giraffes, flatcars that carried spring-loaded helicopters, "television" cars with rotating cameras—the Lionel freight roster contained odd cars that still captivated viewers.

By the late 1950s, the space program had ascended to the top of the news and the Cold War was at its hottest. This was the company's short-lived "space and missile" era, when boxcars hauling ICBMs and flatcars topped with surface-to-air missiles filled the pages of the catalog.

These cars were symbols of their times and of the indecision at Lionel about how best to position its line. The catalogs of those years contained traditional freight outfits, the nostalgia-themed *General*, space and military accessories, and even a pastel-painted set aimed at girls.

By the mid-1960s, the space and missile cars were out of the line. Some of the best freight cars returned, as did the Train Master diesel and the Hudson steamer. Lionel still offered outfits for kids, some reminiscent of the Depression-era Lionel Jr. sets, but its product planners had also taken notice of their adult customers.

1950 Berkshire freight set

The Santa Fe F3 diesel may have been the glamour girl of the post-Second World War Lionel O gauge line, but the rugged 2-8-4 Berkshire steam locomotive was its workhorse. While the Berkshire ranked second to the Hudson in the Lionel steam lineup, that powerhouse was seldom offered. Consequently, the big Berk was the biggest steamer in the line for all but a handful of the years it appeared in the catalog. And while no one is sure which Lionel locomotive was produced in the greatest numbers, this model surely holds the record for longevity, being offered from 1946 through 1968 (though under two different numbers).

With its heavy die-cast metal boiler and frame, in addition to Lionel's top-of-the-line motor, the 2-8-4 was up to any task an O gauge railroader could throw its way. Some early Berkshires boast metal bodies on their tenders, while later models have plastic-bodied tenders. Likewise, some come lettered for the Lionel Lines and others for the Pennsylvania. Though the details on the Berkshire varied over the years it was cataloged—earlier models have mostly die-cast metal details, and later models have a few stamped metal or plastic parts—every locomotive came with smoke plus a whistle (in the tender).

This photograph shows a 1950 Berkshire as the motive power for a freight set typical of that era: a refrigerator car, tank car, gondola, and caboose. Some Berks came with longer outfits, and some were sold without sets. Regardless, each of these locomotives featured that legendary Lionel quality and durability.

freight haulers

The Turbine

When the Lionel introduced its new 20-wheel Pennsylvania Railroad Turbine as the shining star of its 1946 line, the firm showed that it was at the cutting edge of 1940s railroad technology. After all, the mighty Pennsy was the nation's largest railroad, and steam turbine no. 6200 ("the big swoosh") was thought to be the first of many like it. Lionel's new model, scaled to look good with the new postwar plastic cars, offered O and O-27 railroaders a sleek, powerful, smoking steamer to serve as the flagship of their layouts.

Over the next several years, Lionel offered Turbines in a bewildering variety of outfits, from small freight sets through passenger outfits and even in Electronic Control sets. Turbines were everywhere—except, as it turned out, on America's railroads.

The Pennsy's orphan Turbine had not panned out because. while powerful, it was also a fuel hog. The youth of America would never see fleets of Turbines flashing through their hometowns. So, while Lionel's model ran great and looked strong, it also went out of production.

A funny thing happened, though. Lionel had produced so many Turbines and built them so well that thousands of former Lionel engineers had good memories of this unique locomotive. They had such good memories, in fact, that Lionel and other manufacturers have introduced several new Turbines over the past few years. Swoosh!

The Norfolk & Western class J

By all rights, it shouldn't have happened. After all, by the late 1950s, steam locomotives were disappearing from American railroads and the always up-to-date Lionel catalog was showcasing modern diesels and space-themed cars and accessories.

Then came the Norfolk & Western class J in 1957.

With its bullet nose and streamlined boiler, this Northern 4-8-4 looked like the latest in locomotive technology—circa 1935, that is.

Nonetheless, there it was. Even the diesel fans must have admitted that Lionel had created a beauty. Based on the Berkshire, it had a reliable, hard-working

mechanism with Magne-Traction, smoke, and a whistle. Its body shell was a realistic representation of the class J. By happy coincidence, Lionel's existing streamlined tender looked great behind the engine.

In those odd years, however, the unusual was common at Lionel and that included not only the fact that this locomotive was ever built but also the contents of one of the train outfits it pulled. Four of the Super O sets that the J headed were accessory-packed traditional freight outfits, but the fifth featured a full consist of space and missile cars. Well, the locomotive was shaped a little like a rocket....

The FM Train Master

Lionel proudly introduced its model of the Fairbanks-Morse Train Master diesel in 1954 as part of its second generation of post-Second World War trains. Like the new freight cars of that era, the Train Master was larger than any of its predecessors. (In fact, it is a true O scale locomotive.)

The "New Fairbanks-Morse Power Giant," as Lionel described the Train Master in its 1954 catalog, has a finely detailed shell with realistic louvers, see-through cooling grills, and wire handrails. It also boasts two motors, vertically mounted roller-bearing powerhouses, plus Magne-Traction and a horn—it's a Cadillac of the toy train world.

The elegant Jersey Central was the third Train Master that Lionel introduced, after the gray-and-red Lackawanna and the black-and-yellow (sometimes blue-and-yellow) Virginian. The first two versions were sold as freight locomotives and served as the motive power for several sets; the Jersey Central was the headliner of just one outfit—a three-car passenger train cataloged only in 1956—that included the deluxe aluminum streamliners.

The Jersey Central Train Master has become a favorite of collectors and is one of the most valuable Lionel postwar diesels. Lionel did not reissue it until the late 1990s.

IONEL LINES

2056

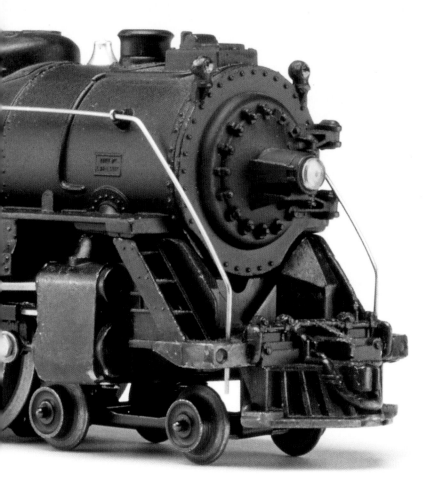

The Korean War

National conflicts have always touched Lionel. Its production of toy trains stopped during the Second World War. The space and missile cars that Lionel made during the 1950s and 1960s showed that it was fighting the Cold War along with the rest of the nation.

The Korean War also affected Lionel. The war began just as Lionel reached its golden anniversary year of 1950 and continued right into the company's peak years. The material shortages plus wartime inflation led Lionel to cut the number of items in its line. The big Hudson was an early casualty, as was the GG1 electric.

Another change that wasn't as obvious from the outside was the removal of Magne-Traction from Lionel steam locomotives for 1952. Because magnets were difficult to obtain, Lionel used them only in its diesels. It still offered a full line of steamers—including Turbines, Berkshires, and small Hudsons—but these locomotives didn't quite have the pulling power of previous years.

Fortunately, these steamers still smoked, whistled, and ran like thoroughbreds. So it's likely that few—if any—of the boys who received their first Lionel that Christmas even noticed the difference. After all, they had a new Lionel under the tree. Nothing could be better.

Coal loading accessories

During the golden days of toy trains, coal was probably the largest bulk commodity to be moved by the real railroads. So, as an adjunct to the operating freight cars that transported and dumped artificial coal on toy railroads, Lionel developed three very popular accessories over the years to load the stuff.

The tall remote-control coal elevator was the longest lasting of these coal loading accessories. Lionel cataloged it from 1938 to 1950—with three of those years off during the Second World War.

"Coal" that was dumped into a bin at one end of the accessory was carried up by buckets on a continuous loop of chain to an elevated coal bunker, where it was ready for unloading down a chute into a waiting dump car or hopper at the other end. The coal elevator was designed for use between parallel tracks.

While the action was fun to watch, it took forever to load the bunker with the buckets, which were rather small and could hold only a few coal pieces each.

So, most young operators "primed the pump" by filling the bunker ahead of time. Then, for effect, they could run the bucket chain only a minute or two before loading the waiting freight car.

The operating diesel-type coal loader, cataloged from 1948 to 1957, worked a bit better than the elevator at lifting the coal and filling the waiting car. However, it had a very ambitious mechanism that tended to spill a lot of coal on the way up.

Patterned after trackside conveyor-belt loaders that were to be found everywhere in the 1940s, the accessory was quite true to function, but it was grossly out of scale—easily three or four times larger than the prototypes. Of course, that never seemed to matter since youthful imaginations compensated for a lot.

It is hard to say whether the last coaling station, which Lionel cataloged from 1953 to 1958, had a real-world counterpart.

Coal was emptied from a side-dump car into a receiving bin at trackside. Then the bin could be lifted to automatically spill its entire contents into a holding hopper over the track. There, the coal waited to be loaded by flow of gravity into another car.

The coaling station didn't take as long to fill as the elevator or spill as much coal as the conveyor, unless the operator had his dump car oriented the wrong way under it. Then the car would unceremoniously dump its load along the track instead of into the receiving bin.

All the coal loading accessories were obviously intended for use on somewhat permanent train layouts. Their operation on living-room-carpet railroads was usually short-lived, with their tenure being terminated by horrified mothers who cleaned up after them.

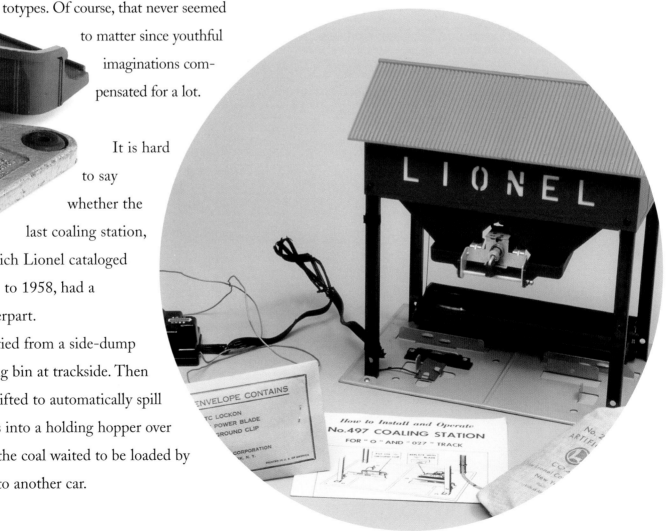

Log loading accessories

These log loading accessories were often preferred over the coal loaders because they were a lot less messy. Little dowel logs couldn't get into carpet fibers as easily as chunks of artificial coal. The action was fun to watch, and these accessories had many real-world prototypes in the lumber-producing areas of the United States.

The chain-drive log loader was cataloged from 1940 to 1950 with three years off for the Second World War. Like the remote-control coal elevator, the log loader was designed to be positioned between parallel tracks.

Logs are dumped from an operating log car into a receiving bin on one side of the accessory. At the discretion of the operator, the logs can be lifted one at a time by a dual-chain conveyor with lumber hooks on it to a holding bin on the other side of the accessory where a pair of stakes holds the logs in place. They can be dispensed into a waiting car on the other track.

The conveyor-belt lumber loader, cataloged from 1948 to 1957, is longer than its chain-driven counterpart. It needs only one track for full operation.

Logs dumped from an operating car at the low end of the accessory can be held there for as long as the operator wishes. When it's time to load an empty car at the other

end, the conveyor belt is switched on and it carries the logs in single file up the ramp to the elevated end. There they usually roll smoothly over three tilting stakes and onto a waiting empty car. A spotting light at the low end indicates when the conveyor is running.

Because there is only one track involved for this loader, operators can use the same freight car at both ends which makes the whole operation seem pointless. However, make-work jobs were so plentiful in Lionelville that they seemed normal.

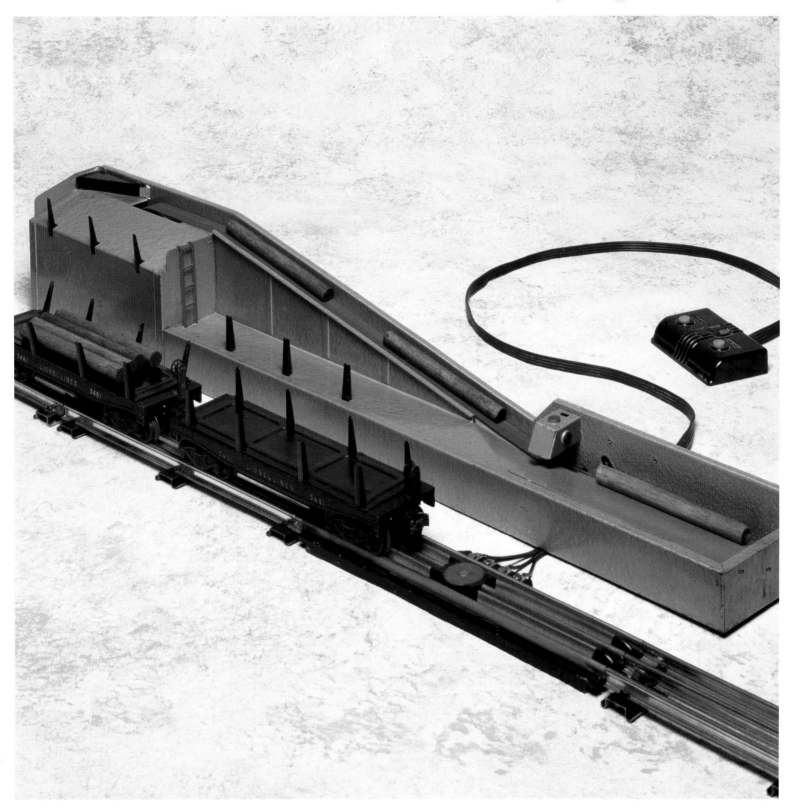

Operating water tower

Steam locomotives always required a handy supply of
water, so Lionel offered several water towers over the
years, starting with a diminutive sheet-metal and brass
model first cataloged in 1931.

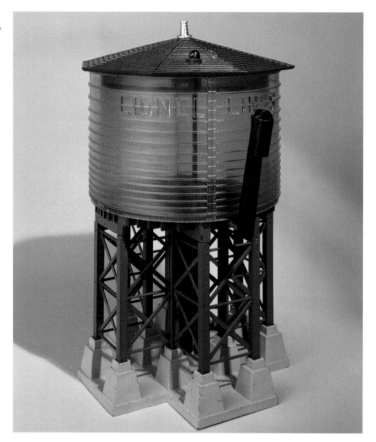

    The most familiar of Lionel's different water
towers is this large operating one. At the
touch of a button, the spout lowers, suggesting
that water is being loaded into the empty tank
of a waiting tender.

    This accessory was cataloged with some
variations from 1946 to 1950 and again from
1953 to 1957. It has subsequently been reissued.

Operating oil derrick

The oil-pumping derrick was a fascinating
industrial accessory that didn't have a
companion car associated with it,
probably because it was difficult, even
for the highly
creative crew
in Lionel's
engineering department, to imagine the kind of action
an operating oil car might have. So they passed.

    A walking beam under the authentic-looking metal
drilling rig simulates the motion of pumping oil from
the ground while heated liquid inside an illuminated
glass tube bubbles merrily upward. This great effect
was no doubt inspired by the bubbling Christmas tree
lights of the 1940s.

Triple-action magnet crane

The triple-action magnet cranes represent an ingenious feat of toy train engineering. Without question, they are the most fun to operate of all the Lionel trackside accessories because a degree of skill, acquired only through practice, is needed to make them work as advertised.

The magnet cranes cataloged prior to the Second World War (1940-42) differ in appearance from the post-war models (1946-49). Prewar cranes are equipped with yellow and red metal cabs; the later ones sport larger black plastic cabs. The booms on these magnet cranes are different too, although the operation is identical.

With four buttons and a switch on the controller, the cab can be rotated 360 degrees, the block and tackle raised or lowered, and the electromagnet turned on and off. A handwheel at the end of the cab raises or lowers the boom.

The magnet cranes loaded and unloaded scrap metal from gondolas. Kids found other uses for them.

Semaphores and block signals

In the pre-electronic communication age, semaphores and block signals were the primary devices that railroads used to prevent accidents by warning engineers of potential dangers on the track ahead. With a system of colored or positioned lights and/or movable arms on structures elevated high above track level so they could be seen at a distance, they alerted train crews of conditions down the pike that required attention and possible action.

Manual semaphores were early Lionel accessories in this category. By the late 1920s, they were electrified and block signals with colored lights were added. These wonderful trackside additions to the railroad atmosphere were triggered automatically by the passing of a train or the presence of another train in the block ahead. On more sophisticated model railroads, the signals could be wired to stop an approaching train to prevent a rear-end collision.

However, all of this was beyond the needs of most operators. They just liked to sit back and watch the blinking lights and moving arms.

Operating cattle car

Following closely on the heels of the automatic refrigerated milk car, the operating cattle car was introduced in 1949. About the same size, it also uses an elevated trackside platform—this time a cattle pen with movable gates—to serve as a stage for the activity.

The scenario is fascinating. Little rubber cows are made to enter at one end of the double-door cattle car and run around the track in the car for as long as the operator wishes. Then the cows exit the other end of the car and return to the cattle pen platform. With more than one car and platform on a layout, cows from one pen can easily be transported to another one.

Traveling aquarium car

The traveling aquarium car probably represented the ultimate flight into fantasy land. It looked much like a boxcar, but had four large transparent windows in its sides so people could see the cargo it carried—all manner of "exotic fish" obliviously "swimming" in their tank as the car moved along the track.

The fish were painted on an endless loop of celluloid that was driven by a small motor and illuminated from within. The windows were made of wavy plastic to enhance the swimming motion. The whole illusion was quite effective, although reactions to the car were quite mixed when Lionel introduced it in 1959.

Boxcars

Early Lionel boxcars looked good in their bright colors, but during the late 1930s and 1940s the company's emphasis on realism led it to paint most of its boxcars in a realistic but drab oxide red (often called, logically, "boxcar red"). Once you had one or two red boxcars, the incentive to buy another couldn't have been all that strong. Realistic? Sure. Boring? Well....

Lionel introduced a new boxcar series in 1953. The plastic models were about an inch longer than their immediate predecessors, making them about the size of the prewar "scale-detailed" cars.

The first few of these cars came in drab colors. By 1954, however, Lionel was introducing cars with three- and four-color paint schemes, and those were just the beginning. By the time the last of the cars in this series was introduced in 1962, Lionel had offered this basic car in green, blue, orange, silver, yellow, mint green, red, and black, plus some multicolor varieties—literally every color of the rainbow (plus black).

Now Lionel railroaders had a reason to buy more than one boxcar—and they did. Even today the cars remain so popular that not only do collectors study their different variations, but Lionel has reissued every car at least once. Colorful boxcars have become as much a part of Lionel railroading as a smoking steam locomotive.

Automatic coal and log dump cars

These, the first fully automated freight cars, were initially cataloged in 1938 to go with the new remote-control coal elevator. They could be filled with artificial coal and made to dump their loads into a trackside bin or at the rear end of the elevator to recycle the action. These red, somewhat top-heavy, sheet-metal rigs were an immediate hit.

The configuration and look of these fascinating freight cars changed to a more prototypical one in 1946. That's when Lionel introduced a heavier vehicle with a better, simpler mechanism and the words "Automatic Dump Car" stamped on the sides.

Although not the first off the assembly line, this version of the coal dumper became the classic. It was cataloged by Lionel for 10 years, after which a longer plastic car equipped with two bins replaced it.

As with the automated coal car, Lionel produced a sheet-metal version of the log dump car during the late prewar era. First cataloged in 1939, this operating car was designed as a natural companion for the chain-drive automatic log loader accessory that was introduced a year later.

The log dump car also underwent an upgrade in 1946. Lionel engineers improved the mechanism and then made the car heavier by substituting a die-cast metal frame.

This familiar model of the log dump car was produced in great quantities during the 10 years that it was cataloged. Then Lionel replaced it with a longer and lighter car made out of gray plastic.

Automatic merchandise car

The automatic merchandise car has the kind of action that makes playing with toy trains such a delight—it is realistic, yet has a larger-than-life quality about it. Designed to simulate packing cases being unloaded from a boxcar as was common at the time, the car's mechanism was overly ambitious and hurled the boxes much farther than would have been possible in the real world—about 50 scale feet most of the time. The freight handler inside must have been a giant.

At the touch of a button, the car door opens and six tiny crates are ejected, one at a time before the door closes. An operator can reload the car by dropping the crates into a trough through a hatch in the roof.

The first version of the automatic merchandise car was offered in some upscale outfits from 1939 to 1942. Updated versions of this boxcar—one a scale model and the other much smaller—were available in freight outfits and for separate sale in 1946 and 1947.

Remote-control helicopter car

One of the more unlikely loads found on Lionel flatcars has to be a functioning helicopter. Actually, it isn't just a chopper being transported; the flatcar serves as a launching pad for it.

The operation can be triggered remotely by the electromagnet in a conventional uncoupling track or manually with a lever on the car itself. Either way, the helicopter takes off, propelled by its own rotor blades.

The power behind all the action comes from a coil spring inside a flat launching spool on the car floor. As the spool is rotated by hand, the spring winds up tight. Teeth on the end of the helicopter's rotor shaft mate with teeth on the launching spool when the vehicle is in place.

When the spring is released, the rotors turn, and the light plastic helicopter lifts off. On a good day, it may reach four or five feet of altitude before it stalls, often crashing into something on the way down. With no way to control the descent, the little choppers have a short life expectancy.

The remote control helicopter cars were cataloged from 1959 to 1965.

Work cars

Many Lionel model railroad operators considered it essential to have a few work cars on the roster for occasional use during emergencies. Most often seen were searchlight cars, crane cars, and work cabooses. Perhaps for this reason, several sets included one or more of these cars, which were also sold separately through much of the postwar period.

The classic searchlight cars were built upon depressed-center flatcar frames. They were equipped with a simulated diesel generator in the middle (usually orange in color) as well as a searchlight on one end. In some instances, the hollow generator shell conceals a switch that controls the light. The searchlight housing is movable and the light can be aimed on all of these cars.

The model shown here features a beacon that rotates automatically as the car proceeds on its journey. While the purpose of this added feature is elusive—it certainly didn't appear on prototype railroad searchlight cars—it was extremely popular among young operators of three-rail trains. Perhaps they were pretending to search the night sky for enemy bombers or to announce the opening of a new movie theater or car dealership in Lionelville.

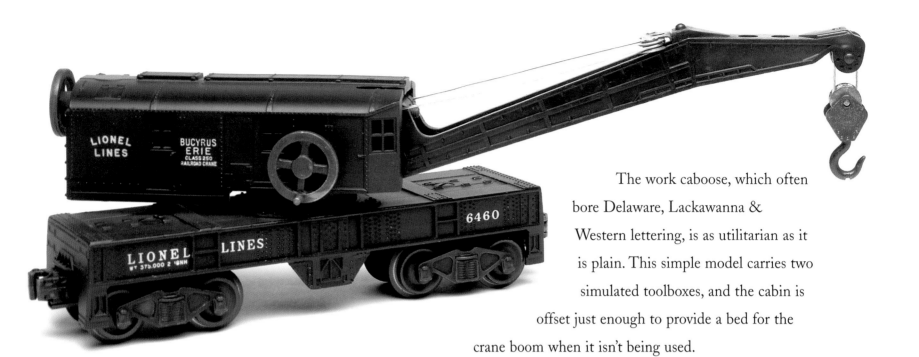

The work caboose, which often bore Delaware, Lackawanna & Western lettering, is as utilitarian as it is plain. This simple model carries two simulated toolboxes, and the cabin is offset just enough to provide a bed for the crane boom when it isn't being used.

All three of the cars shown here appeared early in the postwar period. With some modifications, they remained stalwart members of the Lionel line well into the 1960s.

The crane cars were stout workhorses patterned after the steam- powered Bucyrus Erie products. Both the sturdy boom and the block and tackle are realistically operable by handwheels. Lionel designed the cab to be rotated 360 degrees. That way the cranes can actually be used to re-rail rolling stock, provided an operator has enough patience.

Always workin' on the railroad

*I*n the early years of toy trains, young Lionel engineers (or adult Lionel engineers, for that matter) were on their own when it came to putting their trains to work. On the one hand, imagination was the only limit. On the other hand, one needed plenty of imagination back then. Lionel sold a few accessories, but for the most part the layouts of the era used cardboard boxes for buildings.

By the late 1930s, this situation had changed. Operating trackside accessories added life to Lionel layouts across America. Log loaders, coal loaders, operating bridges, and cranes—along with that perennial favorite, the automatic gateman—all appeared in the catalog.

These accessories varied widely in scale—some were close to O scale, some were more appropriate for Standard gauge, and some were just plain huge—but they were sturdy, reliable, and fun.

When the Second World War ended and toy train production resumed, Lionel brought the best of its prewar accessories back into the line. But planners at Lionel began to introduce new accessories that merged the latest in plastic technology with traditional Lionel mechanisms—plus a large dose of fun.

The earliest new postwar accessories (like the conveyor log and coal loaders and the unreliable pumping water tower) resembled their prewar predecessors in that they were more industrial than whimsical. But the next group of postwar accessories combined realism with whimsy in such engaging ways that they appealed to young Lionel railroaders, their fathers, and perhaps the company's most important customer: Mom.

What made the difference? Men. Little blue men, to be precise. Nearly every one of the accessories that Lionel released in its postwar burst of new items included a figure or two. Some were large, and some were small. Some had painted faces, while others were all-blue (from working in a refrigeration plant, perhaps?). But each of these figures added the special charm that transformed Lionel trackside accessories from electromechanical wonders into something more.

As the years passed, so did life in Lionelville. Piggyback loading ramps and forklift trucks entered the line, models of the new types of freight-handling facilities that were becoming commonplace on the real railroads.

Not every one of these classics (many of which were reissued in the 1970s, '80s, and '90s, some multiple times) included a figure, of course. None of the coal loaders ever did, nor did any of those accessories that handled logs. They probably didn't need them, though, because of the amount of time you could spend with them. Dump the logs, and load the logs. Load the coal, and dump the coal. Thanks to the ingenuity of the designers,

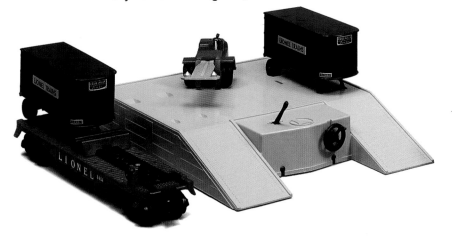

the load/unload cycle could go on indefinitely. (Had the Lionel Lines been a full-sized railroad, it would have been bankrupt in short order, because, while it hauled load after load of freight, the freight never actually went anywhere!)

Other model train companies made accessories as well, but the unique genius of Lionel engineers lay in the number of different ways they worked the busy blue citizens of Lionelville into the line. Didn't want the operating freight station? How about a nice newsstand instead, complete with moving figures. Couldn't quite swing the operating dispatching board? Perhaps your paper route money would cover an operating switchman or a gateman.

The automatic gateman, with his red-and-white shack, is perhaps the most popular of all the postwar accessories, both in terms of the number produced and the smiles caused. When a train approaches (or sooner, depending on how one adjusts the track contactor that activates him), he positively bursts through the door, with his lantern swinging. Then, when the caboose has passed, he scoots back into his shack to await the next train.

Actually, the gateman usually waits for the same train as it runs lap after lap. Still, as long as a young Lionel engineer doesn't tire of the repetition, neither does the gateman.

The gateman, switchman, and crossing gates were actually part of a remarkable series of train- and traffic-control accessories that Lionel manufactured. With several different styles of gates, flashers, and even a clever "banjo" crossing signal with a stop sign that swings back and forth, train-car collisions in Lionelville were certainly not due to inadequate crossing protection.

Layout builders who wanted to have a signal and train-control system that was like a real railroad's could build one using Lionel components. Lionel even worked with paperback publisher Bantam to produce a book (called *Model Railroading*, logically enough) that showed how to combine relays with Lionel track and signals to create a system where the trains would follow each other without colliding, gliding to a stop at the red signals and accelerating smartly when the light turned to green. (You also could do that using the track contactors that came with Lionel signals, but the potential for an unfortunate incident was far higher because the contactors required careful and frequent adjustment.)

In fact, a layout builder could purchase everything for a layout except the paint and plywood from Lionel. On the back pages of the annual catalogs, one could find tunnels (a favorite since the early years at Lionel), a variety of realistic bridges and trestles, billboards (another favorite that today provides a fascinating glimpse of life during the postwar era), sawdust "grass," telephone poles, and more. Coincidentally enough, those pages also included layout plans with lists specifying the number of pieces of track one would need. Track may not have been especially glamorous, but it was one of Lionel's real strengths. It was also one of its greatest advantages over its smaller competitors.

Even Lionel O-27 switches were top quality; O gauge switches from this era are legendary for their reliability and durability. These switches, with their heavy Bakelite housings, are nearly indestructible and include Lionel's famous non-derailing feature, which prevents trains from travelling through a closed route and lets anyone with an interest in wiring create elaborate layouts on which the trains will magically change their routes. Plus with Lionel track's three-rail construction, reversing sections require no special precautions.

As with the Lionel freight car roster, the accessory line of the late 1950s and early 1960s reflected Cold War uncertainties, with heliport missile launching platforms and an exploding ammunition depot. Those items didn't remain in the line for long, though and, as we'll see, when Lionel got back to full speed in the 1970s, the accessories it reissued were not the space and military items, but the newsstands, icing stations, and other classics of the 1950s. After all, they're the real legends of Lionelville.

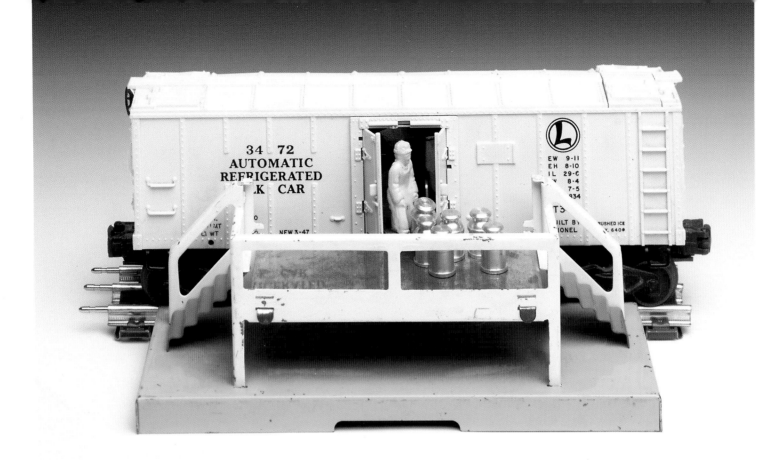

Automatic refrigerated milk cars

At the top of the popularity list among Lionel operating cars was the white milk car. In at least three different variations, it was in the catalog for more than 20 years, starting in 1947, and reportedly sold several million copies.

When everything works right, the milk car is truly a joy to watch. An operator starts by loading the aluminum-colored milk cans through a hidden hatch in the car roof. Then, at the touch of a button, the car doors swing open and a white-uniformed milkman places the cans one at a time onto a trackside platform. (Riding in a refrigerated car, the poor guy should have been wearing an overcoat or parka, but he never did.)

Then the milk cans can be delivered by truck or some other means to their ultimate destinations at the discretion and imagination of the operator. The milk car was—and still is—a very interactive toy, long before most people had ever heard of the word.

Animated gondola

Although this car was cataloged for only two years in the late 1950s and returned for one year by popular demand in the early 1980s, it has made a lasting impression—one way or another—on almost everyone who has seen the thing work.

It's difficult to say just what got into the drinking water at Lionel to inspire someone to come up with the idea of having a railroad cop endlessly chasing a hobo around a stack of wooden crates in a moving gondola car. It's a scenario straight from old Hollywood comedies, combining the Keystone Kops with the Marx Brothers.

The animated gondola not only shows the inventive technical genius of the people who worked in the Lionel engineering department, it provides a glimpse of what might have been at the bottom of the idea barrel at the time.

Operating boxcars

These boxcars provided a way for Lionel to put an "operating car" in an outfit at little cost. The action is simple, minimal, and strictly mechanical—no expensive electrical components involved. At the touch of a button, the car door slides open and a little rubber man inside comes to the doorway. That is it.

There are two notable exceptions to this basic routine. They are embodied in the operating mail car and the operating chicken car.

The man in the mail car holds a mailbag and tosses it to the ground when the door opens. The bag is kept in place by a small magnet, which isn't strong enough to hold when the mechanism jars at the end of its cycle.

When the door of the chicken car opens, the man inside, who holds a broom, begins to sweep out whatever dropped to the floor during the trip. His action continues for a few seconds because he is suspended on a music wire, instead of being rigidly fixed.

The operating boxcars were made in two sizes and featured several different road names. They were first cataloged in 1949 and continued through 1960.

Motorized units

The most fascinating and enduring of the little motorized units that Lionel introduced in the 1950s were the yellow-and-red Birney trolley and the orange section-gang car. These would automatically reverse direction when they ran into an immovable object, such as an end-of-track bumper or a train.

The trolley had interior illumination and silhouettes of passengers in the windows. The trolley pole would whip around as the car changed direction. These cars usually saw service on single-track lines with bumpers at both ends.

The three-man gang car provided a kind of comic relief. Two of the figures were fixed, gazing out from the sides of the car. The third, probably the driver, would turn around when the car collided with something. But he never faced the direction the car was heading until it reversed itself. Then he'd turn around to see what they had hit! Could the names of these figures have been Curley, Moe, and Larry?

Automatic gateman

The most charming and enduring of all the Lionel trackside accessories was, and still is, the automatic gateman. Cataloged for 50 years, long after such railroad employees had disappeared from the real world, the device was copied by all the other American toy train producers and foreign manufacturers in Europe, Asia, and even the Soviet Union. This simple action figure, who lives in a trackside shanty and comes out to wave his lantern to alert motorists of the approaching train, has become the most popular toy train accessory in the world.

The Lionel gateman came to work in 1935 and remained steadfastly at his post until 1984. But his retirement didn't last long—he came back three years later and has been in and out of the catalog ever since.

After 15 years on the job, the gateman's shanty was rebuilt in 1950 of plastic instead of sheet metal. That modernization was the only structural upgrade to this, the longest lasting of all the Lionel legends.

Operating switch tower

Modeled after the type of two-story switch towers that can still be seen on many American railroads, this illuminated accessory activates two men at the same time. As the train approaches, the man standing on the balcony goes into the building, while his partner scurries down the outdoor staircase. After the train has passed, they return to their original positions.

With a double dose of the kind of activity provided by the automatic gateman, only closer to scale proportions, the switch tower was probably intended to replace the oversized man in the shanty. Needless to say, it never has.

Lionel cataloged the operating switch tower from 1953 to 1957. It has reappeared several times since.

Operating freight station

The Lionel operating freight station resembles the familiar style of small combination freight and passenger stations found at waysides in many parts of the country. Typically, these structures are part building and part platform, often with a roof covering both.

The crowd-pleasing action is provided by two empty baggage carts that race noisily out of the building, tear around the platform, and head back into the building again, usually at a speed that suggests their drivers are being chased by demons or are, at the very least, late for supper.

The station was cataloged from 1952 to 1957 and has been reissued from time to time.

Animated newsstand

Patterned after the type of news vendors' stands that could be found on many street corners in America's large cities in the postwar era, this accessory is a whirligig of activity. A newsboy bundled up against the cold waves a newspaper as he turns from side to side. One can almost hear him shout, "Extra, read all about it." The proprietor of the newsstand paces nervously back and forth inside his dark green shelter. Meanwhile, a little black-and-white dog circles the corner fire hydrant as he looks for the right place to pause during his morning "walk."

The action is driven by a single vibration motor and a pulley that is attached with a string to a series of levers, gears, and a rack and pinion. Lionel's engineering department worked overtime on this one.

It was cataloged from 1957 to 1960.

Since such newsstands were rapidly disappearing from the scene by 1988, when Lionel decided to reissue the accessory, it was converted into a white refreshment stand with a twirling ice cream cone replacing the dog and two happy kids in place of the newsboy. Somehow, it just wasn't the same.

Contemporary LIONEL® TRAINS

The key to the success of Lionel during its first 70 years was its uncanny ability to build trains that were robust, attractive, and absolutely compelling to young people. The key to the company's success over the past 30 years has been its ability to adapt its trains so that they appeal to adults via a combination of nostalgia and technology.

Some of the products of this era have been reissues of favorites from the 1930s, '40s, and '50s, while others have been entirely new. In fact, many of the newest Lionel products offer a combination of details and features to satisfy even the most serious model railroader, but with the company's traditional sturdy construction. For those hobbyists who want their Lionel layout to be detailed and realistic, this is a new golden era.

And yet Lionel didn't turn its back on selling trains as healthy, wholesome toys. After nearly starting over from scratch in 1970, Lionel currently offers a line of O gauge outfits that includes a combination of the most popular trains of the past and the most modern trains on America's rails. With new cars, new transformers, and new track, plus the unmistakable "Lionel look," these trains are still making American children happy at the holidays—and all through the year.

BACK TO WHERE IT STARTED

Nostalgia, innovation, and technology

The 1970 line was far from Lionel's most impressive. The catalog was short enough that it fit on the back side of a poster, and the only new items were paint and lettering variations of items from former years. But within this humble assortment lay the seeds for not only a rebirth but a new direction. In addition to its traditional starter sets, Lionel offered a group of boxcars that it labeled a "famous name collector series."

Over the next few years, Lionel would extend that line and introduce other, similar lines that it also targeted at adult consumers. Lionel was returning to an approach that it had largely forsaken after the early 1950s, that of offering an entry-level line for young people and a more elaborate, more realistic—and yes, more expensive—line for adults.

During this period, the General Mills conglomerate produced Lionel trains under license in a former Ford parts plant in Mount Clemens, Michigan. General Mills changed the colors of the train boxes from the famous orange and blue to red and white. It also changed the logo to a more stylized font. For better or worse, this was a new Lionel.

By 1973, the catalog cover showed not only the traditional father-son combo but Grandpa as well. Clearly, General Mills was targeting a market that ran from ages 6 to 60. That year's catalog offered some surprises, including new passenger cars modeled after a type built in the 1920s—an odd choice when appealing to kids, but not if one were hoping to sell trains to nostalgic adults.

The trend toward offering two lines—one for young people and one for adults—only accelerated during the remainder of the 1970s. Lionel reissued a group of its most collectible and highest quality items from the 1950s in each new catalog and also introduced outfits with a variety of new themes, ranging from the Spirit of '76, Mickey Mouse, and Lionel 75th anniversary sets to new passenger sets. By 1979, Lionel had reintroduced nearly its full line of 1950s-era locomotives, including the F3 diesel, GG1 electric, small Hudson steam locomotive, and Train Master diesel.

By 1980, the split was complete. That year's catalog

was in two distinct sections, one for toy trains (called the "traditional line") and one for adults (called, not surprisingly, the "collector line"). Which section came first in the catalog? The adult line, of course. The toy line was sold using the slogan "More than a toy, a tradition," and that section of the catalog used a beautiful illustration of a boy dreaming of a train as its introduction.

By 1982 there were two catalogs, one for the traditional line and one for the collector line. The action-oriented starter outfits included Halloween and military-themed outfits, while the collector items remained mostly reissues of the company's better 1940s and 1950s items. The upper-end Lionel trains of this era featured good quality, solid 1950s-style construction, and paint and lettering that were far better than the work done during Lionel's golden era.

Once a toy train company that also sold some trains to adults, Lionel by the 1980s had become a company whose primary business was making trains for adult hobbyists and also selling some trains for children. The company's marketing paradigm had changed as well. From its birth through the 1950s, it sold its trains with the promise that a Lionel would prepare a young person for the challenges of the modern world. Now its key marketing message was that a Lionel would help adults recapture the carefree fun of youth.

General Mills' production of Lionel Trains ended in 1986. Another toy company, Kenner-Parker, produced the trains for a year. Then, in 1987, shopping center magnate and Lionel enthusiast Richard Kughn purchased not only the license to produce Lionel trains but also all the intellectual and physical property of the train line. His new firm, Lionel Trains, Inc., was fully independent. Operating the company from a perspective that only an avid hobbyist could have, Kughn was free to experiment as he wished and manufacture the items he most wanted to see.

Fortunately for Lionel, the trains that Kughn wanted to

see were also those that his contemporaries wanted. The first catalog of this era, issued in 1987, included some new items, including a big new 4-8-4 steam locomotive. By the next year Lionel offered a stunning reproduction of the O gauge Hiawatha of the 1930s. Soon after that Lionel introduced a new line of scale-sized steam locomotives, a reissue of the scale steam switcher of the 1930s, and more reproductions of classic metal Lionel trains.

Each year brought improvements in some areas, including a more extensive line of track and switches. The track line now included the prewar O-72 switch and O-72 curved sections, which let operators build layouts with curves that were now gentle enough to accommodate the largest O gauge locomotives.

The biggest changes of the post-1970 era, however, came in technology. Lionel designers improved on the technology they had inherited. The freight and passenger cars now rode on a new type of wheel that rolled much more freely, and the axles no longer required lubrication. Beginning in 1971, selected steam locomotives included electronic sound systems. Called "Mighty Sound of Steam," it wasn't exactly Dolby digital, but it was a start.

Even the old reversing units began to disappear as Lionel replaced them with electronic units. At the same time, Lionel began to expand its use of direct current, can-style motors in place of its standard "universal" motors. (A universal motor will work on both alternating and direct current.)

When coupled with an electronic reverse, these motors could be used with standard Lionel transformers. They offered a number of advantages; they were quieter, drew less power, required less maintenance, and were less expensive.

The most dramatic new development is TrainMaster Command Control. It combines a handheld radio throttle with a base station that relays commands from the throttle to the train via the track. In this system each locomotive has its own receiver and unique number, so an operator can control many locomotives independently on the same track.

The system includes a digital sound system, called RailSounds, which reproduces the sounds of the specific locomotive the model is patterned after. Musician Neil Young, a Lionel operator (and later part-owner of Lionel) spearheaded the development of the system, which debuted in 1995.

With these new systems, Lionel was back in the position it had enjoyed in the early 1900s: it was at the leading edge of toy train technology. Remarkably, Lionel engineers managed to do this while maintaining compatibility with its older products. You could operate Lionel's latest on a layout that used a 1939 Lionel transformer and 1915 Lionel track, if you wanted to.

Under Kughn's able leadership, Lionel attained a level of financial success it had not enjoyed for decades. Profitable and reinvigorated, it attracted the attention of the investment firm Wellspring Capital, which purchased it in 1995. Under Wellspring, Lionel has continued on the course set by Kughn, with new technologies, new trains, and even new scales—Lionel reentered the HO scale market in 2003.

Today, more than 100 years after its founding, Lionel remains an American institution. The Lionel name is still one of

the most recognized brands of any kind in the American marketplace. Furthermore, the association between Lionel and Christmas remains as tight as ever. A train under the tree is as much a holiday tradition as a wreath and holly.

While not every American boy dreams of a Lionel of his own, plenty still do, and so do their fathers and grandfathers. Lionel trains, it turns out, do bring families together, as was promised in so many of the famous Lionel advertisements.

The "Spirit of '76" diesel

Remember 1976, when fireworks and commemorative items could be found everywhere and television showed myriad "Bicentennial moments"? The success of the gold Chessie Geep offered in 1973 had convinced the Lionel marketing team that adults would buy toy trains. Logically enough, they began looking for other models to offer, and a bicentennial model was a natural. Even better, the real railroads had done the graphic design work for them! Nearly every railroad eventually had a bicentennial-themed diesel, with the most famous being the General Electric diesel that

the Seaboard Coast Line painted red, white, and blue and then sent on tour.

For its 1974 line, Lionel developed a new O gauge locomotive, its U36B, and offered it in bicentennial paint that matched the Seaboard's design (as catalog number 1776, of course!). Lionel fans could, over the next several years, add a caboose and 13 specially painted state-themed boxcars to the set.

A commemorative of one of the country's biggest celebrations at the time when it was issued, the set now celebrates the rejuvenation of the toy train hobby.

1984 Hudson

As Lionel regained its strength through the 1970s, it began to reissue many of its legendary trains of the 1940s and '50s in updated versions. Enthusiasts began to wonder when Lionel might reissue its biggest post-war legend, the scale-sized Hudson, which had last been offered in the mid-1960s.

Then, on the cover of the 1984 catalog, it appeared. The Hudson was back, and it wasn't simply a reissue. The 1984 had an improved smoke unit, more magnets for better traction, electronic sound, and a metal

tender, which had not been issued since 1950. It was a beautiful locomotive, and it ran like a fine watch. That wasn't all. The catalog also included New York Central freight cars and two-tone gray NYC streamliners.

Lionel released two modified versions of this Hudson shortly afterward. Then came a reissue of the magnificent scale Hudson, complete with a scale-length tender and Rail Chief cars. Together, these locomotives showed the world that Lionel was truly back at the top of its postwar form.

The Santa Fe, circa 2003

A near-constant in the Lionel line since 1948, streamlined Santa Fe diesels have been a barometer of the company's technological prowess—and its health.

The first Santa Fes were the legendary F3s, which had two horizontally mounted motors, one in each truck. In 1950 Lionel added Magne-Traction. Three years later it switched to vertical motors and deleted some details. Next came a single-motored version. The Santa Fe F3 survived into the 1960s, although most of the units sold were smaller and less expensive Alcos.

By the mid-1970s, the Santa Fe F3 was back minus Magne-Traction and packing only one motor. As Lionel regained its strength, so did the F3. The second motor returned, as did Magne-Traction. By 1996 the Santa Fe F3—still based on the 1948 tooling—had first-generation digital sound and TrainMaster Command Control.

With the market moving toward bigger, scale-sized locomotives, Lionel introduced a new scale-sized Santa Fe—an Alco PA passenger diesel. Then Lionel added to the O-27 line: a new Santa Fe FT diesel. The FT was the predecessor of the F3 in real life.

In 2003 Lionel introduced its newest Santa Fe F3. The model's TrainMaster Command Control, smoke unit, RailSounds, and Odyssey "cruise control" system raised the bar for manufacturers of streamlined diesels.

1948

1996

2003

EPILOGUE

In the history of American industry, very few products have achieved the longevity—more than 100 years—as well as the immediate name recognition and respect that Lionel has enjoyed through many generations of customers. Perhaps "fans" may be a better word, for enduring support and almost unconditional brand loyalty indicate strong emotional involvement with the trains.

Why? Surely, the role that railroads played in American life was a key factor. Possibly even more important was what long trains pulled by big, powerful locomotives might have represented in the hearts and minds of young boys. Perhaps the appeal had to do with father-and-son bonding or the wish fulfillment that comes from finally owning the dream toys of childhood. Maybe the trains evoked warm images of home, hearth, and family together at Christmas. Then again, it may have been all of the above.

As soon as it became socially acceptable for adults who didn't necessarily have children in the household to own and operate Lionel trains, the floodgates opened. Most people started out by collecting a few of their favorite pieces. Because the trains were designed to run, the next logical step was to have some sort of layout to showcase the collection. From that point to building an elaborate model railroad was usually a very short step.

Today's Lionel trains employ cutting-edge technology in their motors, their electronic "TrainMaster" control systems, and in their digitally recorded onboard "RailSounds," which faithfully play back synchronized echoes of prototype locomotives in action, realistic in every respect except decibel level. These features were created in recent years for men who like to have toys within their toys.

Painstaking attention to detail and carefully applied paint and lettering give contemporary Lionel trains character equal to that of the models usually found in museums. The line between "toy" trains and "scale" trains is getting thinner and less distinct every day.

In what hobbyists call the "modern era"—the 34 years from 1970 to the present—Lionel produced more than twice as many trains and train-related items than it did during the previous 69 years, which included the so-called "Golden Age of Toy Trains." This alone is proof that the nostalgia-driven adult market is alive and well and has a voracious appetite for variety. Surely the millennium has arrived, and it took only 100 years to get here.

A visionary in the Lionel advertising department coined a slogan back in 1956 that became a prophecy. It foretold the role that his company's products would assume in the future: today's world of the adult collectors. For just as his slogan said, Lionel trains were and are "a lifetime investment in happiness."